And Then Em Died...

Stop The Insanity!

A Memoir

by

Susan Powter

Table of Contents

CHAPTER 1

Dear Em,

We lived in a lot of places, you and I. The last few places I stayed after you died I couldn't and wouldn't have stayed with you. They weren't safe, not for you while I worked all day and not for me, but I had no other choice and you were dead.

I had no place to go after I got the notice that the RV parking spot we'd only just pulled into three days before; was it the Wednesday of the Saturday that you died?

Either way, it was within days of the move from one RV parking lot to another. One that was our home for the last five years, and one that was as far from that as I could ever have imagined.

It was only a few days before we had to move that I first noticed something was wrong with you.

In the middle of our walk, the loop around the RV park we'd taken twice a day for years, you pulled to the side and lay down on the dirt under the row of bushes that line the entrance to the park connected to the casino.

You lay down on the dirt.

That was the only sign I had that you'd be dead within a few days and that everything in my life was about to change forever.

I can't tell you exactly how many days it was after I drove back from the vet without you, but it was very soon after, a day or two, that I got a knock on the door of the spot we'd only just pulled into. It was management telling me they were re-paving the parking lot and everyone would have to leave in a few days.

A few days after you'd died, just after we had moved, I had to move again. Move with no way to. No way to tow it, no way to pay for it, and nowhere to pull it to; nowhere to live.

KOA...

We'd only just left KOA, our spot for years on Boulder Highway, our home. We had to leave because we were kicked out.

I remember getting the notice on the pod door that November telling me we'd have to leave in March of the next year, four months away. Corporate's new rule. All RVs or campers over 10 years old had to leave.

I was shocked and embarrassed once I figured out that they had been walking past for the last few months scoping out people they wanted to get rid of.

I was hurt that I was one of them, that we were on the list even though our 1950s Aristocrat camper clearly fell under their new rule.

Admittedly, I could understand that they wanted to get rid of most of the RVers who'd been living there for years before we got there, but not us.

People Who Lived There...

Within the first few days of pulling in, I met the guy with two rigs up against the back wall. His wife, his 2-year-old son and him.

Mister always had an opinion, a complaint, gossip about everything going on in the park. The stories of the disability system screwing him and his never ending family fights were as constant as the mess around his rigs.

Evel Knievel's son lived next to the left side wall for years. The tales of his drinking were notorious with casino security saving him time after time. He left a few years after we pulled in, got arrested in Arizona and died.

The lady with so many cats they had to call animal control, they trapped 17 from her tiny rig.

The guy behind me, living in a pop-up tent with his children "visiting" more than they were living with their mother. He was always there right behind us living his life outside his camper.

We had absolutely no outside anything, no privacy for a few years, but KOA was home to me. It was safe. As safe as inner-city living could be in one of the worst neighborhoods in Vegas.

Casinos don't mess around with their security. What they want is people staying and gambling, so the safest you can be is near a casino in Vegas, certainly if you're living in an urban RV parking lot.

Living there was community to me. It meant the way I still want to live: in an RV park with people coming and going every few days. In Vegas it means people from all over the world visiting, thrilled to be there. I loved that. It was our home.

The way we were living was still an art project to me then, Em, not poverty. I never once believed I wouldn't be able to work my way out of, back to ...

I loved our corner RV slot a few slots down from the office, right next to the bathroom. And I loved, though I disliked many of them, the daily KOA staff that ran the park.

Bill, the head of maintenance. It would be hard to describe what a perv this ex-Navy, "nothing he couldn't fix," guy was. He loved us. He loved you Em, and you loved him.

Bill, who never listened to a thing I said about feeding you everything he had on his cart for the park dogs, always saving the best for you.

Bill, who every time he passed me commented on breasts, butt, anything and everything I wore. Sexual workplace any of it meant nothing to him. Bill, the drinker he was, never missed a day of work.

His daughter worked in the office and lived against the back wall near the second set of bathrooms. If anyone knew everything that was happening in the park, it was him. Any and all of what went on at the park Bill knew, and he told me.

Then there was Mr. Security, who figured out who I was before anyone else did. Mr. Gun-carrying, zealous Tea-Party-member who still lived in his mother's house in the same neighborhood within a few miles from KOA since he was born.

He stopped by, unsolicited, all the time. I was always on the lookout for him, learning his shifts so I knew when he'd come by, closing the curtains or pretending to be on the phone.

But when and if I ever needed security, and I did, there was no better pissed-off, ready-to-pull-the-trigger guy than him if he liked you. And there were, still are, all the regulars ...

Frank, from Canada, who pulled his rig into the same spot, catty-corner from us, every November through March. His wife was the kind of gambler casinos love. Every season for years Frank was as much a part of the park as the staff in the office.

Every day on his way to get coffee at the casino at 5 a.m. and me getting ready to go to work, we would chat for a few minutes; we were friends.

He continued to call my number a year after we'd been kicked out, for a year after you were dead, Em. I never answered, I couldn't, what would I tell him?

Boulder Highway, as dangerous as the neighborhood is, that road meant something to me.

Every day I drove to much better neighborhoods to work and every day I drove home down Boulder Highway knowing the history of it.

I knew it was the original road — they all drove this road when they came to Vegas. Marilyn drove this road. I knew the history of these outlying casinos before they got to Vegas. The strip didn't exist; what is downtown Fremont Street today was the Vegas they drove Boulder Highway to.

I knew the "Welcome to Fabulous Las Vegas" sign within blocks of us was the original sign designed by Betty Willis, who considered her sign a gift to the city.

She never had it copyrighted. It cost $4,000 to build and she never saw a penny from it. Maybe that's why that sign meant so much to me.

KOA was home to me.
It was safe.

Urban RV casino living in Vegas — that's what it was when we pulled in and within a few years it turned into a corporate upgrade.

They got rid of us bit by bit, weekly pay increased and soon turned into monthly pay. Corporate started walking past and I got a notice in November, three months before we had to leave, enough time if I'd had any idea where to go or how to pay for it.

I remember that afternoon, scared to death, talking to Mary whom I worked with, on staff, cleaning the bathrooms in the park to lower my weekly rent. Mary who couldn't understand my fear that day.

Mary, who could not see an eviction notice as anything other than normal, having moved every six months since I worked with her. I know because I moved her. I had a car, she didn't; she had three kids to move from weekly to weekly at least three or four times while we worked together.

Mary, who always said she was "staying at" not living in; the first time I realized what that meant. Mary was sitting at the kitchen table unfazed by the injustice I felt that day and my fear.

The March deadline came and went, they gave us a few extra weeks to move because we were different Em, they did like us, but corporate is corporate and we had to move.

KOA to Circus Circus...

Chris, the KOA manager, towed us to Circus Circus that day. I was so grateful to him; he was very helpful and kind, I was so obviously out of my league. Unplugging the pod I was embarrassed about my bitten-to-the-cuticle nails and only just beginning to be embarrassed by my whole life, only just.

You jumped into the car just like you'd done since the day I got you from the pound 10 years before and we followed him to Circus Circus, but it was so obvious something wasn't right.

It had only been a day or two since you'd started lying down on the dirt during our walks, but we had to move and I had no money to do anything let alone pay for a vet bill, and to this day I think you knew that, my love.

Chris waited while I checked into that office, the polar opposite of KOA.

He pulled the pod into the slot at the back of the parking lot, up against the wall just off the Strip. I promised him a pizza would be delivered to the office in the next few days to thank him, and he left.

And there we were. There I was, lost. There was no green anywhere. No corner spot. No trees, no bathroom anywhere near, no security, no real food for miles, and you were dead within a few days.

The Day Em Died...

I only worked my morning shift that Saturday and came back to get you because I knew you had to get to the vet right away.

You'd had trouble stepping from the pod on your walk the night before, and that morning you'd lie down again, this time in that trash-filled strip of dirt behind our pod. It was our last walk before that walk into the vet's office, an hour later that Saturday morning.

With no way to pay, I Googled a vet open on weekends, thinking you were sick with something we could and would fix.

I drove out of Circus Circus on that road, Bridge Road — I only just the other day noticed the name years after you've been dead, driving past it almost daily to deliver on the Strip, and every time, to this day, I say out loud in tears still much of the time, "I love you, Em!"

It was in the parking lot of the vet's office when I went to help you out of the car that I felt it. I'd never felt it before, not the night before, not weeks before, that massive lump on the side of your neck.

You could barely walk through the doors, and as soon as we got into the lobby you lay down on the floor. It was the last time you ever walked, Em.

She was lovely, the vet. She listened to me, took you into the back room to run some tests until she very quickly, too quickly, came back and said, there is no point in running more tests.

I was on the phone asking my son for money to pay the vet bill to make you better, to do whatever I needed to do to fix whatever it was, when she walked back in and said, "Cancer is everywhere."

She brought you back in on a blanket and left us alone while she went to get the shots.

I sat on the floor hugging you, sobbing, stroking your velvety ears, and telling you what a magnificent dog you are, were, always will be, how much I loved you, and what you meant to me.

And even as sick as you were, whap, whap, whap, your tail thumped the floor when she walked back in with two syringes on a silver tray: one to sedate you and one to kill you.

You whapped your tail just like you did when I walked past your stall at the shelter the day I adopted you. The way that made me stop and go back to the stall you were in.

You against the wall not up against the cage door barking like every other dog, you whapped your tail then just like you did when she walked in. She gave you the sedative and gave us a minute.

"I love you so much, Em," I said sobbing, kissing your big head over and over again. "I love you so much," like I still say out loud, out of nowhere, always, "I love you, Em."

I held you and you died.

"Please treat her well," I said sobbing as the vet dragged your body away on that blanket, it was only then I realized what it was for.

My son called and paid the $500 bill, and I left without you. An hour-and-a-half after driving you there you were dead, and I was driving back to Circus Circus without you.

Within a few days I got a knock on the door, management letting me know they were repaving the park and everyone had to leave.

Within days of you being dead, within a few weeks of just moving, I had to leave again. I had to leave with no way to, there was no RV park manager to help me, I didn't know how to find a tow truck for the pod or where to tow it. It was one of the first of many times I felt desperation.

Downtown Fremont...

I have no idea how I found the tow guy, but he showed up the day I had to move, with his very pregnant wife in the passenger seat of his tow truck.

He charged me maybe $50, $75, and little did I know that we would be towing friends through the birth of his child, through him towing the pod to storage and months later owning it.

I sold it to him for $200 after it had been broken into and destroyed (in storage) by a meth addict, he totaled two RVs and the pod, little did I know, a whole lot then ...

But the first time he towed the pod was within a week or two after you were dead, Em, and he towed it to that horrifying spot under the bridge in Fremont.

I remember one of the RVers at KOA telling me about a park he'd stopped at once on his way to Vegas, a place under the freeway I'd driven over enough to see the parking lot below.

That's where I went. He towed the pod, I followed. He pulled me in, hooked me up and left, and it was horrible.

From our spot at KOA to Circus Circus without you, Em, to a place that didn't even pretend to be anything other than a parking lot, with a few bathrooms in the middle of the worst part of downtown Vegas, and no security at all.

That place, those bathrooms were so dangerous. There was nothing I recognized anywhere near me. There was no food for miles, and what I had to walk past every time I went anywhere for anything was unimaginable, and then, the car.

The car my son bought me five years before and had delivered to me with such love and excitement started to break down. That car was freedom to me when I got it and never more so than when my only source of income was/is dependent on a car.

The car that I loved and needed started to break down, which meant no work, which meant only the beginning of trying to get the car to the mechanic for days, sometimes weeks at a time with nothing to do all day, every day until it was fixed, and that happened over and over again.

One of the last times I took it to the dealership before my warranty expired, the 60-plus-year-old service man said to me, "You can't expect it to last more than five years."

This was just after he'd mentioned his daughter was pregnant again and that she needed to "tie her ankles together from now on," and I said nothing.

I said nothing because I wasn't in a position to say anything. I've never said nothing in my life anytime a man says something as — you fill in the blank — as that, but I was so desperate to get the car fixed and get back to work so I could make up for the morning and lunch shift I'd lost.

I knew it was the last time I had the luxury of a warranty. That day I looked and felt old, tired, out of place with all the people busy living their car-maintenance lives. From that horrible place under the freeway something started to die in me.

The car breaking, no money, no real food, no security, no RV community, no you, Em, no nothing. It was there that my life started to change forever because I did.

I stopped believing that working hard enough could get me out of this. It was there my dreams started to die, and it was there my family started to change forever.

I don't know how long I was there, maybe a few months, I had to leave because of some monthly rental increase above and beyond what I could pay.

I had to store the pod. There were no other RV parks to go to. When I found out I had to leave KOA, I'd looked into all of them, from the very best to the worst of the worst, so I knew I had to store it and find a place to live, and my only option was a weekly rental.

I called my tow guy, his baby born by then in her car seat in the back. He hooked the pod up and again I followed him, this time to a storage space.

He pulled the pod in up against the back wall and he left. Something there, in that moment, in that place was different.

I felt alone and scared in a way I'd never felt before. It was desolate.

I literally had nowhere to go that afternoon. I had no credit. No money. Nowhere to go so, I drove to Harbor Island.

Harbor Island...

A weekly a few blocks from the Vegas strip. I knew Harbor Island because I had picked Jay up for work there, and I had also driven his girlfriend to his place after their madly-in-love, passion-filled, alcohol-and-meth-infused fights.

The kind of love affair I recognized, but on a whole other alcohol-meth-infused level. You'd think those two words alone, alcohol and meth, would be enough to conjure chaos, but no, when I say alcohol, I have never, and believe me I have.

I have never seen, every day, all day, Big Gulp cups full of vodka at 7 a.m. I have never seen such massive amounts of it all: vodka, whisky, xanny bars, weed, every pill under the very hot Vegas Strip sun.

I worked with Jay as one of the most despised people on the Strip. Timeshare salespeople, I was the stopper for some of the best salespeople I have or will ever know.

I needed a job. I needed to get paid daily, and I applied for everything. I interviewed to be one of the characters in costumes you pay to take photos with.

I interviewed with Chewbacca and his friends. That day I realized I was out of my league; I felt stupid. I knew they laughed when I walked away, I knew I didn't have any idea what hustling on the Vegas Strip was/is. All the things I felt that day that I didn't know, within a few months I did.

I knew Harbor Island because most of the people that I worked with on the Strip stayed there. I knew Harbor Island because Jay got kicked out of there.

I came to get him that day, and to be kicked out of there meant he had? I can't imagine what he did, I didn't ask.

I never thought living at KOA in the pod that it would be a possibility to have no place to go, without you, Em, other than Harbor Island.

I'll never forget the first time I pulled into the parking lot, that space in front of the office. The same office I would go into to pay my weekly $200, plus the $11.95 surcharge; $211.95 for longer than I ever imagined possible.

But that first day I was desperate to rent a room. I was scared to death and mortified. That day in the office, filling out the forms at the desk, I was afraid.

Afraid that my credit rating, which was and still is nothing, would mean I couldn't get a room that night, a place for a week, a month? A place to live.

I had no idea what I'd do if I couldn't. I hadn't spent months studying stealth car living then, nowhere near it. I was so alone and afraid that day and soon found out that nothing made a difference at Harbor Island, a bad credit score the least of it.

I got a room (the first of three rooms there) and I moved in with my wool blanket, a pillow, a sweatshirt and a pair of sweatpants.

*My first room
five doors down from Elvis.*

Yes, Elvis. You've seen this Elvis if you've been on the Strip in the last 10 years.

The Elvis on his red electric scooter, always with a massive can of beer in his cup holder working the strip seven days a week from 9 a.m. to 2 p.m., and he drank and drank and drank.

I'm sure he's still working the Strip, a different spot now, things have changed since I worked there, before that young woman with her baby in the back seat drove up onto the sidewalk and mowed people down.

I went down to the Strip the morning after that happened and videoed Doc the homeless guy who lived on that corner and was as much a regular, allowed to live there by security just like the time-share people and the costumed characters were allowed to work there before that happened.

Elvis was the first person who drunkenly yelled at me one day, "Hey, you remind me of that lady on TV, remember her? Do you remember her?"

"Remember, she had crazy hair," he screamed, like only a drunk at 10 a.m. can, and he wouldn't let it go. I left that day and avoided him for months until he had forgotten he'd ever remembered me from somewhere, until ...

Until I came back to my first-floor room one day, rounding the corner, I saw him. I saw him scooting down to his room, five rooms from mine and I was horrified.

I turned around before he could see me, and I ran. I ran from him. I ran from the shock and embarrassment of being one of them. I ran from the reality of me having no choice but to live there.

What is intrinsically hysterical; living five doors down from Elvis in Vegas was not funny at all. It was terribly sad.

That first room was more dangerous than the next two, because a ground floor room meant there was nothing more than a window (they didn't even have to climb stairs) separating me from every day at Harbor Island.

The First Room
Building C, Room 128...

I had nothing.

There was nothing to move in, but I had a kitchen, I had a TV, and I had a place to stay. I was grateful to be somewhere.

There was no real food for miles, but I had two legs that worked. Urban food desert, all the (awareness) rage right now, and it's real. CVS a few blocks away was the only food I had for the first few months.

It's a horrible walk through that parking lot, over the Vegas tunnel people, the sights, the sounds, the smells walking to CVS to buy food.

From that room, the man above me lost his mind. He screamed for hours while the cops did what they do and the crowd of people gathered below to film him on their phones, to laugh at him, it was amusement for the afternoon, something to do in a place where disaster is constant.

Like the morning the dead body in the room across from me was being taken out at the crack of dawn. I was shocked at the amount of prescription pill bottles lined up outside, along with his dead body under the sheet, and everything he owned in full view while they took their photos of the death scene.

Maintenance wasn't even a consideration. Everything broke, there wasn't a thing that didn't need something. The only things that got maintenance to come were major like my bathroom ceiling falling through three times.

The guy upstairs passed out in the tub, and after the third time in the middle of the night —not a few drips, not a slow leak; no, water raining down and chunks of ceiling falling in the bathroom — I had to move.

From that room, my car broke down for good. After whatever repair I'd waited days to get done, within a few days another warning light, the transmission this time so, no point fixing it. My son said, "Find a buyer who can fix the transmission and sell it," and I did.

From that room, my grandson was born 1,125 miles away. From that room, after a month or two of walking to CVS for food, once I realized nothing was going to change anytime soon, I started walking to get real food.

I didn't calculate how many miles it was (turns out it was eight); I knew how far it was there and back based on how impossible it felt every day that I did it.

I got up at 5 a.m., Sprouts opens at 7 a.m., thank God — I walked there and back. I only shopped for one-or-two-days' worth of food for two reasons.

No money and walking eight miles there and back carrying groceries but, the food I made in that room. The smell of it!

The woman next door leaning against the wall smoking her cigarette every time I saw her mentioned how good the food smelled coming out of my room. It was a moment. A moment between two women living in that horrible place.

From that room I walked to the welfare office to get insurance. I badly needed dental work. I'm grateful to say I have never walked into a welfare office in my life, and I never want to again.

I'll never forget that walk back. Something changed in me. My dollar-store flip-flops melted under my feet walking back. I was so sad and as hopeless as I'd ever felt in my life.

It was so hot, so far to walk, so many people zooming past, living their lives. I could not believe I was walking from the welfare office I'd just spent all day in, to the welfare weekly I lived in.

That sentence alone ...

I sold the car for $1,500. I met the buyer in the parking lot and sold it. That $1,500 was all I had to live on until my son bought me another car and I could get back to work.

The only thing I bought when I sold the car was a bike from Walmart. A bike I could ride to get food. I walked there that morning, bought a bike and a lock and rode straight to Sprouts.

I remember that first bike ride of far too many, back to Harbor Island balancing grocery bags on the handlebars, exhausted and shocked but thrilled to have real food.

On the days I just couldn't ride that far, I rode to the 99 Cents store. I rode very early in the morning to avoid seeing anyone else shopping for food at the 99 Cents store. A horrifying place to buy food but it was better than CVS.

Months later those bike rides were almost impossible for me. They were so long, so tiring. To this day I can't drive a few of the streets I rode then with grocery bags balancing on the handlebars, knowing how far I still had to go, stunned and exhausted.

I had to move from that first room after the bathroom ceiling fell through for the third time. And management put me first on the list, only because the women in the office so appreciated the most basic respect.

I moved to the second room at Harbor Island. A third-floor corner room. I'd learned by then that a corner room was a luxury, nobody on the right side of me, so there was "a window you can open" the office woman said to me as she was showing me the place.

Other than my whole life and real food, one of the things I missed the most was fresh air, any air, so being able to open a window was, and is, a luxury.

I lived there for months and would have stayed in that room until he moved in underneath me. I lived there through however many people came and went downstairs — a few months turnaround is normal in these places — until he moved in and never left.

It's not about the noise in places like that. It's not about the daily fights or people leaning/nodding against your door or sitting all morning at the top of the steps with a six-inch knife waiting for ... someone? Not anything I was willing to walk out of my door all day, until he left, to find out.

It's not about the sights and sounds of the daily/weekly horrors, never more so than a few city blocks from the Vegas Strip. I waited months for him to leave or die; the amount of drugs and alcohol (redundant) he was doing every minute of every day would have been enough to kill anyone, except him.

After months of security being called about the level of noise, violence, banging, crashing, throwing, fighting, the parties, day and night, the language, the anger, the hatred, the horror, it made no difference.

It's hard to describe the danger when everyone he invited over, who missed the second versus third floor, knocked on my door at all hours of the day and night. It never stopped.

It was from that second room my son bought me a car. He called to tell me he would buy me a plane ticket so I could go and pick it up. A perfectly normal thing to do, except when it was impossible to imagine.

Flying to Seattle...

Flying for the first time in more years than I thought possible and flying with nothing. I felt subhuman. I felt as if I didn't belong.

I didn't have any of the things everyone around me had. Normal traveling people and their things. And then there was me. Normal things were beginning to be impossible to think of ever having again.

It was very difficult seeing my son for the first time in a few years. It was awkward, something that was unimaginable to me.

I remember looking at his teeth, the dental work he could afford, and thinking we lived in different worlds now. I was embarrassed about the position I was in and felt like I was dying inside.

My grandchild was six weeks old. It was the first time I'd seen him. I saw him for a few hours and went to the gas station with my son to fill up the car so I could immediately start the drive back.

It was there, while my son was filling the tank, that I knew that everything in my life that meant everything to me was changing.

It was uncomfortable. It was forced. We were different, he and I. Something had changed. It was impossible to understand.

I got on the road and drove 24 hours straight with only a two-hour nap and a huge cup of gas station coffee. That trip was exhausting and frightening. There was a construction stop on the highway, and I didn't know how to restart a hybrid car; I'd never driven one before.

Cars were speeding towards me at 70 miles an hour, I had no idea how to put it into gear. I was panicked. The construction guy waving the cars around me to stop them from plowing into me was yelling at me, "There's something wrong with your gears, something's wrong with your car," the car I'd just picked up.

I got back to Harbor Island the next morning at 5 a.m. I started delivering with a vengeance, day and night. After months of waiting to be able to work, with the fear, boredom, hopelessness and exhaustion that I could barely make it through every day, I had a chance.

I had renewed hope that I could work my way out of this, that I could work hard enough, deliver enough to begin to get the most basic things I so that desperately needed.

I was still staying in the second room waiting for him to move out. It was intolerable. It went on for months, day and night. It was so dangerous, so defeating.

The few times I called security, when they finally showed up, all I heard was dude, bro, yuck, yuck, yuck. I went to the office with videos, it made no difference, there was nothing I could do.

I had to move, and the next place I got was one of their "renovated" units with an increased weekly rate I couldn't afford. The same office woman showed it to me with pride and a guarantee I would not have the same problems in this building.

I moved from one building to another again. Up and down three flights with a few boxes each time, hopeful.

And that third, newly renovated room was the worst of them all.

Every move was hard. Walking up and down stairs from building to building with the few things I owned. I felt completely alone. My back hurt, there were buildings full of new neighbors' eyes on me as I moved in.

I never touched the carpet without shoes on in any of those places, never slept on one of the beds. I only ever slept on the disgusting sofas covered by my wool blanket.

That third space was the most horrifying and it was impossible to believe. It was a shock to me because I knew there was no place to go if I couldn't live there, and there was no amount of cheap gray vinyl tiling and the sloppiest renovation you've ever seen that could change the two things that were impossible to live with. The new noise and the roaches.

The New Noise...

The man underneath didn't work and rarely left his place, and he had a massive gaming system up against the wall. Day and night my walls vibrated with video war games like I'd never heard, and the roaches.

I've lived in Texas and New York City so I know roaches — flying roaches in

Texas — but I've never lived anywhere where I'd put a spoon down on the counter on a plate, walk back seconds later, and find six roaches on the plate, never.

I had no food in the cabinets, everything in the fridge was covered in plastic, and my place was clean. There was nothing I could do about the roaches.

I went to sleep every night, on the sofa, never the bed (not those beds) dreaming about roaches crawling in every room, because they were, it was disgusting.

I was so defeated, so tired working all day every day for what ended up always amounting to just over $10 an hour, trying to get somewhere, anywhere, and I began to give up.

The weight of it, can't catch a break no matter how hard I work, coin it any catch phrase you'd like, it's a very real atmospheric pressure that crushes everything.

The up-against-the-odds that made me begin to forget me. The years and years of my life before Harbor Island started to disappear.

Everything, in my life for 60 plus years before, not just the money, everything started slipping away. I was shocked and confused every day by everything.

I had to move, and my only other choice was another weekly complex — or to try and get an apartment, and the few times I'd tried it was impossible with no rental history, no credit, no anything.

Senior Living...

I'm writing a memoir, Em ...

I titled it: And Then Em Died with three dots that follow because what's happened in my life since the day you died is the story of my life before you, a life millions of people knew and it's the story of my life now, a life nobody would believe; a life that's impossible for me to believe.

I'm writing my memoir standing at the kitchen counter in the place I'm staying for the next six months. A place I got into by the skin of my teeth. No, I got in because of my gift of gab and the $2,500 my son gave me.

I found a 55 and up, senior apartment complex in an old school, North Las Vegas neighborhood. Single units, what a luxury, a porch, beyond a luxury, and so, so quiet.

I talked my way into this place. My energy overwhelmed/charmed the woman who's been running it for 30 years. After all these years, Em, my energy still is.

"I last rented from Harbor Island," I said, and she literally clutched her pearls and said, "Oh my." I talked my way into first, last, and deposit and, I could pick up the keys a few weeks from Tuesday.

It was when I was moving out of Harbor Island not just from floor to floor, building to building this time, carrying the few boxes I had to the car — I felt it.

I felt the fear and desperation that comes with having nothing. Not having the most basic things to plan for, take care of, move forward in any way but, I was so grateful to be moving into a clean, quiet place.

I had absolutely nothing. No bed, no TV, no clothes to hang on the no coat hangers, and no money to get anything. I was frightened, alone and so aware I had nothing.

I'm writing the story of my life, a memoir from a kitchen counter that is lifesaving to me right now. Fingers to keyboard all these years later, after how many books written? A lifetime before us, Em.

I couldn't think about writing this book, not only because then versus now was impossible to think about, to feel, to write, but also because the most basic things I needed, things I never thought I couldn't get if I needed; like glasses to see the screen of this very old computer and internet, there was no chance of getting.

Trying and trying, and I did, wears you down. No matter who you are, no matter what your circumstances, no matter how your life may or may not have worked out. It wore me down, even though it took years.

There certainly was no chance of writing it while I was simply trying to survive every day, every month, every year, for more years than I ever thought possible. I couldn't understand it, let alone write it to the world.

Until now. Everything is still barely working, from my glasses to this old computer and the car, always, barely working, 240,000 miles now and still delivering 8-10 hours a day, every day.

But now every other day after my shift I stand in this kitchen and write down my memories. My story. The sequence of events in my life, just to remember so it's documented, for my memory, for me.

I'm writing about my life now, from this kitchen, Em, a life before you. The life millions of people knew, a life that started in a kitchen in Garland, Texas 30 years ago.

Stop The Insanity!...

You know the story. You certainly do if you are forty years old or older and if not, your mother does. The prince walks out, single mother, two babies a year apart, 260 pounds, lost the weight, i.e., Stop The Insanity! the very beginning.

I had no idea at all about the possibility that anything close to what was about to happen could. What I did know as a single mother of two in Garland, Texas in 1984 was that I was financially doomed.

I looked into weekly childcare, and I knew I was screwed. I had to figure out how to make the most money in the least amount of time, paying a babysitter to come over so I didn't have to put my kids in daycare.

So, I went to work stripping. Stripping in Dallas, Texas in the '80s. I hired (and paid more than she'd ever been paid in her life) a young Christian woman as my nanny, and I went to work, dayshift at the strip club, 11 a.m. to 7 p.m. every day.

I became Bernadette in a parking lot of a German Bakery around the corner from the strip club. I pulled in just before every shift, put my wig and make up on, and went to work.

When I was on stage I wore long floral dresses, Stevie Nicks' "Leather and Lace" was my music, unheard of in the '80s strip club anything. Billy Squier's "The Stroke" was the standard stripper music in the '80s.

I worked the day shift; I was there with my kids when they woke up and was home to make dinner and put them to bed. And I made very good money.

The only person who knew what I was doing was my father. I told him in case something happened to me after booking a private bachelor party on some ranch in the middle of nowhere, Texas.

Other than everything about it, it's good work. Totally different in the '80s or not? I'm not sure, the last strip club I went to was in New York City, years ago.

I danced my shifts, took my cash and went home. One day there was a table full of executives to the left of the main stage. I remember wearing a dress with a petticoat, a Laura Ashley print, on the main stage, dancing slowly.

One of the men at the table tipped me a few hundred dollars on the first stage and followed me to all four stages, tipping me $900. More than I'd ever made on one set.

When I got off stage, I went to the table full of his top executives, who were celebrating whatever it was they were celebrating, men I would soon get to know very well.

I thanked him, introduced myself, and went back into the dressing room and didn't come out again. A few days later he came back. Within a few weeks he asked me to go to Mexico on a corporate trip, and I did.

And, of course, when you become their girlfriend, they don't want you dancing in the club anymore, which means they pay the bills, and I stay home with my kids, which is exactly what I did, and I started teaching aerobics.

I started teaching aerobics in Dallas in the '80s. My first time as an aerobics teacher was at the very expensive Premier Club, where my boyfriend was a member. The very beginning of a career I had no idea was about to be.

You can't imagine how seriously this exercise staff took themselves. The certified aerobics experts in the late '80s, every club claiming they had the best of the best, and then there was me.

My classes were packed. I brought my two kids, they sat and played while I worked. My music was fabulous. They gave me the class slot that had no chance in hell, 4 p.m., before the 5:30, 6:30 classes their star teachers taught, and my classes were booked beyond capacity.

After a couple of months, I was called into the office and fired. I was fired because I "explained too much to my class." "We just need you to hype them up, not teach them anything." "You're just a bit too much for our club."

My stripping career ended when I broke both my feet in half falling off the main stage when some idiot thought it would be cute to pour his beer onto the stage. At the hospital, the intake guy clicking away on his keyboard asked what I did for a living. "I'm a dancer," I said. He looked down at my two obviously broken feet and said, "Not anymore," as he clicked away.

My strip club boyfriend and I broke up. I was raising my two children, moving on from my first marriage with no desire to meet anyone, and ...

No need to do anything other than list the circumstances of my very brief, second and last marriage, except to explain how it's connected to me opening my first exercise studio.

I met him in Dallas just before I was moving to Tucson. Getting away, fresh start, easier cost of living, small-town Tucson at the time. He showed up at my front door in Tucson one afternoon and asked me to marry him.

I had just moved, unpacked, cleaned, and organized a whole house with two children while I was teaching aerobics full-time. He showed up for a visit and a proposal and immediately dumped his things on the floor.

I distinctly remember looking down and knowing the disrespect and complete lack of understanding of all the work I'd done; red flag, what you'd call it now, the first of many, and I still married him.

I lived in Tucson; he lived in Dallas. I moved back to Dallas because he asked me to after months of long-distance living. I knew I had to find a way to make a living. I knew I was going to teach exercise and, after working in a few places, I knew I had to start my own studio.

So, I made a deal with the prince sitting outside on a curb and laid it out. He would be my childcare, I would pay him, and I would start a business that would support all of us — an exercise studio. I rented a duplex and moved my ex-husband in downstairs, we lived upstairs. Far beyond conscious uncoupling or co-parenting, and I paid for it all.

My First Studio...

I decided to open an exercise studio with no degree, no certification, no nothing except the only thing I needed. Everything I had done to lose over 100 pounds, everything I'd learned, everything that pissed me off that I had found out along the way.

Teaching women everything I knew while I taught them how to move properly: form, resistance, control, and extension.

Teaching women to reconnect their brains and bodies, how they could love the way they look and feel.

There was a space already set up for an exercise studio that had gone out of business. "Why would I rent to another exercise studio?" the landlord asked. I said you won't lose any money renovating it to be a dress shop or anything else if you give me a chance, and I talked my way into a lease.

I owned an exercise studio, The Susan Powter Studio, in one of the three most competitive aerobic markets in the country — New York, Los Angeles, and Dallas.

Aerobics/Dallas/the '80s,
it's a genre.

I was up against the most competitive, heavily funded studios and instructors with every certification you could ever have, with no idea at the time how far they'd go to try and destroy the success that nobody ever expected possible, success I never thought about or planned.

I had a business to build, a chance to make a living for me and my kids, and I loved teaching wellness. First thing; the class schedule. The same as every studio was and probably still is.

- 6 to 7 a.m.
- 8:15 to 9:15 a.m.
- 12 to 12:45 p.m.
- 4 to 5 p.m.
- 5:30 to 6:30 p.m.

The same as every other studio in town, except I was the only teacher. I was the only everything. Front desk, teacher, cleaner, runner of the studio, me.

I taught 20 classes a week and bit by bit, it didn't take long before the Dallas aerobic elite, front-row women found out about my classes. They never missed a class, and their spot was their spot once they claimed it.

If two words sum up Texas in the '80s, it's big hair. And then there was me, bald. I taught those classes with energy that brings tears to my eyes as I write about it so many years later. It was fierce. I'm super proud of that 30-something woman who poured her heart out in every class.

That front row the day Ellen showed up. The Dallas aerobic weight-loss queen. Years of trying everything to lose weight, every program, every method under the sun. I'll never forget Ellen in the front row that day in the original studio taking the 8:15 class.

I'll also never forget Ellen showing up that Sunday night at the end of another exhausting week. I was mopping the lobby floor and remember looking up and seeing her, getting out of her car, walking towards my closed studio door with food.

Pulling up because she knew I was exhausted, and she knew my husband was useless. She said, "I knew you'd still be here working, I brought you some food," and she took the mop from my hand and finished mopping while I sat and ate, and we talked and talked and talked. Our conversations about books, always, poetry, and fitness. I loved her.

Then Jill showed up. I was in my office on the phone when the biggest Cadillac I'd ever seen pulled up. A woman with a cast on her right arm stepped out, threw her cigarette on the ground, stomped it out and walked straight into my office with a question about the fat content of egg whites versus egg yolks, and I loved her.

And Sally, not the same as the other front-row women, a corporate professional woman in Dallas, Texas in the '80s. A few weeks after she first took my class, we were in the lobby watching a teacher audition, and I asked her to come and work at the studio

She quit her very high-paying corporate job to come and work for the studio, for me, for what I was teaching, for the energy that was not happening anywhere else. I had nothing to offer her except all that.

At that first studio I started my New To Fit class, an unheard of class in the '80s aerobic scene. I started a class for morbidly obese people because I knew how hard it was to be the only obese person in the back row in an aerobics class.

There wasn't a studio in Dallas where anyone who wasn't brilliantly fit could go. I was passionate about my New To Fit class. It started with four or five people.

Willy, the pharmacist, drove miles to take my class four times a week. Willy, who told me his obesity had shamed him to the point of desperation. He told me he could no longer manage his hygiene, his wife had to help him clean himself. He loved that class, making it very clear he never thought he'd ever have the option of taking an aerobics class until he found New To Fit.

Four classes a week, four to five people and me. Word got out that there was a class for morbidly obese people, and the Dallas press called.

When I say press, way pre-internet and then add Dallas press in the '80s, it's hard to imagine now the power, attitude, and control they had.

The female journalist they sent was not thrilled because they had her on the aerobics beat, so imagine how pissed off she was when she walked into a studio with four morbidly obese people and me.

Without hesitation I said to her: "These people are here to reconnect with their bodies and change the way they look and feel. Please be respectful of our class, you can sit and watch," and I taught my class. The exact same class I always taught. She thanked me and left, and I never thought about it again until the article came out.

I didn't know what the release date was until I was in my office and the phone started ringing and didn't stop for hours. I was there answering every call: "Hi, this is Susan Powter, thank you for calling, give me your name and number and I'll give you a call back within the next 24 hours. Again, thank you for calling."

Not a recorded message on an answering machine — no, I was picking up every phone call, writing names and numbers down on a yellow legal pad, and I called every one of them back.

The studio was growing; I'd hired two teachers and wanted some P.R. to get the word out, to get more people in the door so I went to a local PR agency to have a meeting about increasing visibility for the studio.

I had $3,000 and a $2,500 payroll due the next day; every month after payroll and bills, I was barely making it. That's the exercise studio business.

In that meeting I talked a million miles a minute about modification, fitness for everyone, all fitness levels, the fittest of the fit and new to fit.

I told her how I could teach any fitness level, because I can teach anyone how to modify. Which means anyone can get lean, strong and healthy. She leaned forward and said...

"Do you know you're a good communicator?"

"Yeah, yeah, yeah, anyway, what I want is to tell the world is" ...

"Do you know you're funny?"

"I don't know, never thought about it, anyway, I want to get the word out" ...

"Do you know you are a very good storyteller?"

"No, not something I ever thought about, meantime, what I want to do is get some PR for my studio and my program that I believe so strongly in." I invited her to come and take my class.

*She took my class
and never left.*

Her plan was to book local media to get more exposure for the studio. The first interview was a radio fitness show. First thing I said, sitting in front of the mic, was, "God, look at this big thick thing in front of my mouth," and we were off and running.

At the very beginning of the interview, I saw Rusty on the other side of the glass holding up the cue cards she took with her to prompt clients to help them with their interviews.

I saw her hold a card up for a second and slowly put it back in her lap with a shocked look on her face, a look of recognition that she was onto something with me.

All I knew was that I was dying to talk to everyone who was calling in, and the lines were lit up. I had a fabulous time because I completely ignored Mr. Radio, whatever-the-host's-name-was. I talked and talked to every caller who called in.

Those buttons were lit up through the whole show, and I talked to everyone, loving it, much to the host's dismay. And then came the phone call from Richard Frankel.

Richard had been morbidly obese his whole life, shamed constantly by his very successful older brother, and he had tried everything to lose weight.

I told him about burning fat, increasing lean muscle mass, metabolically the most active tissue in the human body. I told him if you live in a human body, he (any human body) can get lean, strong, and healthy.

I told him if he could curl a five-pound dumbbell, we could; if he could put one foot in front of the other, we could; if he had the courage to show up at my New to Fit class on Monday, we could, and he did. He showed up, and he loved it.

Richard was very bright, he understood the "absolute facts of the burn-fat-if-you-live-in-a-human-body" matter, and he was thrilled. Thrilled enough to tell his brother what was happening, and next came the phone call from his brother, Jerry Frankel.

A well-known, wealthy local businessman. He invited me to a meeting in his office and within a few days offered me a "partnership." The investor who was known for contractually owning and destroying people/women. I had no idea.

"Jerry Frankel wants to invest" is all I knew, and I was summoned to a meeting in a hotel room — him, his three lawyers, and me.

No lawyer, no Rusty, just me, and I signed the contract. A 50/50 partnership to open exercise studios and maybe a fitness clothing line, that's what I went into business with him to do.

The Susan Powter Corporation...

Step one, expansion. The second studio was new, around the corner from my original one-exercise-room studio. It was bigger, with two fully equipped studios, a break room, two offices, one for me and one for Sally, by then my right hand.

We had magical nights there, Ellen, Jill, Sally, and I, breaking down after long days. Drinking beer, singing in the studio, laughing, loving "We Was Girls Together" (Toni Morrison) and I loved it.

The program I developed was a three-month fitness program.

— $350 for all fitness levels.

— A private consultation with me.

— Three months of unlimited exercise classes.

— Three food workshops.

— Three movement workshops.

Ninety days to burn fat, increase lean muscle mass, activate (resurrect) your metabolic rate, reconnect with your body and take your brain and body back.

> — The same blood that feeds your body feeds your brain.

> — Eat, breathe and move.

> — Oxygen is the only thing you can't live without for more than five minutes.

> — You have to eat to be lean.

They understood every word I was saying. They left with a real understanding of how they absolutely could change the way they look and feel forever, and they did.

I didn't "talk too much" in my studio. I couldn't talk enough about burning fat, increasing strength and energy, and getting lean, strong, and healthy.

Those women, those private consultations in my office, the truth spoken, the laughter, the tears, the moments of awakening in that office; I did thousands of consultations.

The lobby became a place women would arrive way before class and stay as long as they could after; a place for women to gather, talk, laugh. They lingered in that space/place before they had to get back to their daily lives for as long as they could, and they loved it. They were fiercely loyal clients.

Something happened a few months into running the new studio that started to change everything, a fluke.

The Home Show...

I was invited to do a segment on one of the last live-audience morning shows on television, "The Home Show," with Gary Collins and Sarah Purcell. I flew to L.A. and was picked up at 4:30 a.m. the next day by the ABC television shuttle.

I knew nothing about TV, the stages set up in that massive room, the cameras rolled to and from each stage for every segment. I was in the green room and called to set.

Gary and Sarah walked over from the segment they had just finished and sat down. The cameras start rolling towards us, Gary looks at me, points, and says, "What the hell is this?" then immediately, "Hi, I'm Gary Collins welcome back to 'The Home Show,' where today we are talking to ..."

The red light was on, which meant we were live. He asked me a question or two, and for three minutes or whatever the length of the segments were back then, I broke every rule in television, certainly '90s morning-show rules.

I looked directly into the camera, leaning in from my stool, and talked a gazillion miles a minute. I talked directly to the women I knew were watching, and I told them about the diet and fitness industry scams. I told them fitness is for everyone, no matter how long it's been, how unfit you are, how, how, how, I told them about:

— Modification

— Fitness for all fitness levels

— Working within your fitness level and building to any fitness level you want to be.

I told them ...

— From new to fit to the fittest of the fit is only a matter of levels of intensity, and any human body can increase or decrease levels of intensity.

— How modification is the only way, and nobody's teaching it, so why wouldn't you feel defeated?

— I told them about form, resistance, control, and extension.

I used real words, not jargon.

I told them everything I'd found out that had pissed me off, everything I did to change the way I looked and felt, and how they can and will, and then ...

I turned back to Gary. I don't remember if I ever said a word to Sarah. Gary said something as banal as everything that came out of his mouth every time he spoke to me, yuck, yuck, "Someone get her another cup of coffee," however he ended, it didn't matter.

I walked off set knowing I would never be invited back, which made no difference to me at all. But I did get invited back. Rusty got a call, "We'd like to have her back because our ratings were ..."

They booked me the week of Thanksgiving when they knew there was no chance in hell any weight loss or wellness segment was going to hit any numbers in the ratings. But it did. Bigger than the first segment, which I found out later was record-breaking for their ratings.

And a call back again the next week, along with a meeting with the head honcho at the time. After my segment, I went upstairs to his office and he said, "We'd like to invite you to become a member of 'The Home Show' family."

"As what?" I said, "The family member you'd never fess up to." Yuck, yuck; nothing, no response at all, and I got the job.

A weekly segment on
"The Home Show."

A very big win for the corporation, not anything anyone ever expected, big, big exposure.

I started my weekly commute from Dallas to L.A. I was running the studio, teaching, raising my children, running a home, doing it all with an ex-husband downstairs and a current husband upstairs, working woman, redundant.

My once-a-week segments on "The Home Show" were the beginning of national exposure. Calls started coming in for interview requests, product offers and appearances.

It was from that duplex that I did the Connie Chung interview, massive national exposure at the time.

And then came the book ...

Stop The Insanity! The Book...

I had a meeting with a legit literary agent, who was working with the biggest publishing houses at the time, an agent Rusty was so jealous of.

The three of us went to New York to pitch a book called Stop The Insanity! with no book proposal, to visit eight publishing houses. All day, from one meeting to another, it was me talking and talking.

Seven meetings and then, the only meeting that matters. Me and Bob Asahina at Simon and Schuster.

Bob and I in his books-piled-floor-to-ceiling office, exactly what you'd expect the office of one of the top editors at Simon and Schuster to be, Bob and I talked and talked.

We talked about the millinery business and high colonics for a lovely few hours, and then I mentioned I was going to write a book called Stop The Insanity! about wellness.

He walked me to the elevators, and Rusty, Jan and I walked back to the pub at the Fitzpatrick Hotel on Lexington Avenue to celebrate a great day of meetings. And I got an offer.

A two-million-dollar advance,
without a word on paper.

As soon as I got back, I started writing my first book. I wrote it from that duplex, from the office just off the kitchen after

Stop The Insanity! A Memoir

the boys were in bed after everything was done for the day.

I started writing it with a ghostwriter, standard practice in the publishing industry, especially when you're talking about an aerobics teacher, writing her first book having just been paid two million dollars, more so than ever a ghost writer was a given, but not for long.

I interviewed however many and settled on Connie-what's-her-name, paid for out of my advance. We met maybe three or four times in L.A. when I was there for my "Home Show" segments.

We'd meet for hours, I would explain everything I'd written that she was about to read, and she would return it with nothing I recognized. Not even close to what I'd written.

After our third or fourth, what would be our last meeting I flew back to the studio and I called Bob. Something, apparently, no first-time writer ever did.

-73-

I didn't go through my literary agent or Rusty, I called him directly from my studio office and said, "Bob, you've just pissed away two million dollars if I can't write my book on my own and, certainly if I have to write it with Connie-what's-her name."

After that phone call I started writing Stop The Insanity! on my own and have every book since.

And still, one year after Stop The Insanity! had hit the New York Times bestseller list, I found out Connie-what's-her-name's answering machine message still said, "Hi, this is Connie, the co-author of Stop The Insanity!"

I wrote my book and then a few months before the final edit, I lost it.

I lost the book.

I was commuting from New York to Dallas, and I left my computer in a bathroom stall at LaGuardia airport. A horrifying feeling once I realized it and knew no amount of phone calls was getting a computer back from an airport bathroom, no flash drive backup happening then. It was gone, so I rewrote it from memory from that studio office.

The Infomercial...

Then came the infomercial. A five-camera, live audience massive shoot and nobody even bothered to ask me what I was going to wear or what I was going to say. Nothing. Nobody.

I couldn't wait to get onto that stage. All I thought about was talking to women, the more the merrier. I never took a note, rehearsed, practiced, or thought about it. I talked for hours and loved it.

When I tell you within the first few minutes of me jumping around in that cut-off sweatshirt and those purple leggings saying what I was saying, I looked down at one point and saw sweat dripping from the face of one of the money men sitting in the front row.

The suits were sweating and losing faith fast that this thing was ever going to be anything.

They never thought it would do anything close to what it did, and it wouldn't have if their final edit had gone to air.

I got a copy of the first cut before it aired, and it was horrifying. They had edited all the truth, the humor, the woman-to-woman out so, I changed it.

At the eleventh hour in the Zig Ziglar (Google 101 early '80s motivational speakers) studio editing rooms, in the middle of the night because it was cheaper to rent then, with reel-to-reel, tape, and razor blades, swear to God editing that way, and it wasn't that long ago.

And then, it aired.

It aired just after Christmas. Just before the January weight loss everything that it still is to this day, and it blew the roof off.

It blew the roof off of the infomercial industry. They'd never "seen a launch like this." It was "breaking records" every day and, of course, they "knew all along" that I was, that it would be ...

The money they were saving on "conversion time" shocked them. "They don't ask any questions, they just say, 'I want it. Whatever it is, I want it,'" they told me, thrilled about what they never expected to happen.

"Saturday Night Live" parodied me just after the infomercial aired. I didn't see it, but the phone didn't stop ringing the next day.

I was still barely married to my second husband with my ex-husband living downstairs and me paying all the bills, and the studio was changing. It was suffering. It was suffering because I was gone more and more commuting to L.A. weekly for my "Home Show" segments.

My weekly commute as a family member turned into a limo picking me up instead of the shuttle bus and having to stay a few more days a week for all the other offers, projects, and meetings that were coming in, which meant weeks away from the studio.

The book was about to be published, and I was called/summoned to a meeting at Simon and Schuster with every head of every department at the biggest conference table I'd ever sat at.

Bob Asahina and Carolyn Reidy were the only two people I knew or had worked with. Then I heard from Carolyn Reidy, the President of Simon and Schuster, "We got a letter; they're threatening to sue if we publish you," and then silence.

And then Carolyn, smoking her cigarette, looked around the table at every head of every department at Simon and Schuster and said: "Look at her, she can tell a story, she can speak, she's entertaining, and she can write. We're publishing it."

I asked for the letter, and I left, then I had it traced. I had it traced from the corporate stamp machine they ran it through back in the not-so-long-ago-day.

It came from a business owned by the husband of an aerobics teacher in town. She and her buddy taught at a competitive studio. It was only the beginning of how far they would go to ...

Then Came the Videos...

Huge, Time Warner — nobody bigger at the time. Fitness videos at the height of fitness video everything. My first, "Lean, Strong and Healthy." The title alone, who was even using those words, and again with the purple tights. The first of however many platinum videos.

I was very busy and thrilled to be, things were happening left, right, and center, far beyond an exercise studio and a clothing line, and nobody was a better team player than me.

I was doing the work to get it all done. I wrote the books, I did the videos, I did the speeches, I did the interviews, I did the TV appearances and after whichever next massive deal we got that nobody expected, I asked for a corporate meeting.

Jerry, Richard, Rusty, and I sat at the table in his office, and I told him I wanted to change the contract going forward.

Everything he signed me up for (the company was making millions and millions more than he ever expected) would stay the same, 50-50, but ...

I wanted to move forward with other projects with a different split. Imagine, I was still willing to give him an unearned, very generous split until, before I finished the sentence he pointed his finger in my face and said, "I own you, if you choose to teach piano lessons, I get 50 percent of you for the rest of your life. I own you."

I immediately said, "Get your fucking finger out of my face before I bite it off," and I got up and left. The meeting lasted a few minutes, I walked out and never saw him again, except in court, in the first of too many lawsuits to count — litigious and the '90s, synonymous.

Where did the money go?

Start at the beginning, at the very top. Padding bills doesn't even come close to what was happening. It didn't surprise me that he was stealing from me, but a racehorse? A racehorse named Susan Powter that I found out about years later. I had no idea. An actual racehorse with my name that was winning races?

If ever there was one of the most expensive (and horrifying) hobbies on the planet Earth, it would be owning race-horses.

There was a massive lawsuit, too many lawyers to count, and it was the end of The Susan Powter Corporation. And then, the biggest deal of all, a TV show, and the beginning of the end.

The Susan Powter Show...

I made it very clear I never wanted to live in L.A. I didn't want to raise my children there, and the only way I'd do a TV show was to live in Tucson and commute weekly to film the show.

"No problem, Suz, we'll shoot Monday through Thursday, it's a short commute, you'll be home Thursday afternoon through Sunday with your kids," so I bought my first and only (ever) house in Tucson.

I divorced my second and last (could I have said last enough?) husband. I told him in Dallas I had gotten the deal for the TV show and that I was moving to

Tucson, and I didn't invite him to go. The marriage had been over for a long time in the very short time we were married.

That move to Tucson was life-changing for me. It was the first time in my life I was living with and around women only, and I loved it. I hired a staff of women and their daughters, staff meaning ...

— Full-time childcare

— A house manager

— A book researcher

— And Sally, always

I paid the father of my children and his horrifying wife to move to Tucson so he would be there for his children and continued paying him to be a father until years later when I stopped.

I was working on another book, launching a national TV show, doing every interview and meeting and shooting videos.

Time Warner came with their massive production trucks sitting in the driveway for days, the production was shut down too many times to remember by the desert sun, something I thought was brilliant for obvious reasons.

That video me, Sally, and some man, Chris something, in the front room of the house. I don't remember why there was a random man in my video. I'm sure it was some Time Warner executive's decision to try and grab the male market, a way to sell more videos.

I was very busy. I'd say this was the height of Stop The Insanity! Nowhere near the most fun, as a matter of fact far from it, not even close to the most productive, but millions of dollars were being funded by massive corporations that controlled every industry I was in.

— Books: Simon and Schuster

— Videos: Time Warner

— TV: Multimedia, Inc.

They owned me and I was beginning to figure it out, but only just beginning to because "We've got a TV show to launch, Suz."

As hard as I tried, some of the things that mattered most to me started to die. It made no difference how many studio OG women's weekends I arranged, things started changing at the speed of light.

There was nothing I could do about it. Those studio OG women, that time, our love and friendship changed my life forever.

What I came home to after exhausting business trips alone — I came home to candles lit, food cooking on the stove, an immaculate house, a hot, essential oil bath being run, hours of conversation/meetings about every detail of everything that had happened. I came home to women.

A community of women — granted, a community I paid for, but a community of women, and I loved it and always will.

I was commuting from Tucson to L.A. to shoot the show Monday through Thursday. Three shows a day, two shows in the can, one to air.

Very soon, four days of shooting turned into five and they also needed me for meetings for the next projects, which turned into we need you in L.A. full time. Less than a year after I'd bought my first, and only, house, I moved to L.A. for the show.

The TV show, where to begin? Let's start with the first meeting we had about where we would shoot the show. The theater on Santa Monica Boulevard that I chose that I was told we'd be shooting in versus the prefab complex that a few days before production began they told me we were shooting in. "The Susan Powter Show" compound they rented.

It was a shock, the first of many, having nothing at all to do with where we'd be shooting the show, having everything to do with how I found out about everything connected to my show.

What I wanted, the energy of, the environment, the hours spent and shows produced from the place to be was:

— A good show, which they never got close to.

— Childcare available for all employees.

— A recycled, environmentally conscious workspace.

— A woman-centered environment, with as many single mothers hired as humanly possible, and on it went.

What I got was three prehistoric old white men who owned, directed and controlled everything I did.

Woody Fraser, Ray Katz, and Herman Rush. Woody and his ass-grabbing, literally every woman who walked within a foot of him. It was beyond belief. HR was nowhere in sight, they owned HR, it was the '90s, not that long ago.

The only house I've ever owned was sold for me, handled by lawyers like my divorce, and I moved into a massive rental house in Pacific Palisades close to the TV studio.

If I had to guess what the rent was? $15,000 a month, something like that, not to mention the monthly maintenance, living, traveling, live-in help, and everything else.

I certainly wasn't paying attention to that because I was working around the clock, and I had lawyers, accountants, and a manager, paid mightily to do just that so, I worked and worked and worked.

I spent 15-18 hours a day in my TV show office, Sally's next to mine with the door open always — until, within a few months of the show, she left. That was the beginning of the end of one of the most organic, passionate, life-changing times in my life.

It was a monstrous deal to get a national TV show. I was offered it, we signed to do it, and I promoted the hell out of it at NATPE.

I went from booth to booth, market to market, station to station, and I sold "The Susan Powter Show." Big celebration, "We got 98% of the markets," everyone was thrilled, "the largest launch since ..."

I was standing in the lobby of the hotel surrounded by every top executive of everything connected to launching a national TV show, and I saw them walking up. From the corner of my eye, a group of men, and I could feel what was coming, their energy was obvious.

"Hey, Bernadette," Mr. good-looking, blond, Texas boy said very loudly, rattling the ice in his glass of liquid courage, and Rusty froze. Here we were at this level of success and having been a stripper in the past was not what it isn't today.

Time Warner, Simon and Schuster, and all the massive companies were still afraid of the press getting a hold of, finding out — nothing I was ever hiding, but they were, certainly Multimedia.

Before he finished getting the name Bernadette out of his mouth, I turned, shook his hand, and said, "Hi, I'm Susan Powter, you must be one of those men who put hundreds of dollars in my G-string, nice to meet you, I'm in the middle of a meeting right now," and I turned around and continued without missing a beat.

There was a palpable respect within our circle for the way I handled it and an obvious slinking away of him and his buddies when his shame game didn't work.

And off we went to the huge launch party and the marketing surprise they presented me, that they'd paid a fortune for a massive glossy box and inside was? Two sticks of dynamite. Pow-Pow Powter, get it? That was their campaign. I was shocked. It was ridiculous.

I hated every moment of "The Susan Powter Show," I hated every segment of that show, and it was then that everything started to change.

Bob Asahina flew to me to edit my next book, Food. I was shooting three shows a day and editing late into the night with Bob. I was working on books, audios, videos, interviews, meetings, and a TV show I hated.

Every effort I made to change it, hundreds of production meetings, shows taped, made no difference. After months of trying, I called the president of

Multimedia and asked him to fly to L.A. and meet with me. Again, apparently not something anyone did and having no idea at the time this guy didn't fly anywhere for anyone.

I met with him in the living room of that rented mansion that my family and I had never living-roomed in. The two of us sat down, and he was fabulous. It was one of the best business meetings I've ever had, and I told him everything.

He asked me what I wanted to do, and I said I wanted out of the show, and it was done. It was the end of the TV show and the very beginning of the end of Rusty and me.

The deals weren't pouring in. We weren't as connected as we'd always been. I wanted less, and she wanted more. I moved from Pacific Palisades and downscaled to Bel Air. I am acutely aware of how ridiculous that sounds, but it was a downgrade.

Rusty's house was just down the street from Barbara Streisand and up the street from Danny DeVito and it was outrageous. The video shoots, interviews, and business meetings she held there with the required house tour before we'd start was embarrassing. That house, those meetings, the deals being made were less and less connected to me in any way.

I'll never forget sitting outside of the massive, sloped lawn with as professional a tennis court as I've ever seen to the left of the plantation-looking monstrosity of a house.

A house costing how much a month? It was just before I had to appear at whatever meeting that day, I was listening to "Tuning My Guitar" by Melanie. A song, to this day, that means a lot to me.

A song I had transferred from album to cassette tape (because pre-internet, can't say it enough in the telling of this story) and it dawned on me. I was the only revenue generator in this company. I was funding all of this. Things that never did, still don't, mean a thing to me.

And the person who represented me, believed in me, was changing. I began to know it on so many levels. There was a moment in the kitchen breakfast nook on a break from filming when some corporate executive was talking about the environmental "issues" and said, "Well, the rivers are being polluted," …

I immediately said no,
and the room stopped.

"The rivers aren't passively being polluted, they are being polluted by men who run the corporations that have destroyed, not are destroying, already have destroyed our planet and continue to do so at a rate that's never going to be able to be stopped."

Which is absolutely true.

Which is who I am.

Which is exactly the energy that got us to that kitchen in that mansion being interviewed that day, and I instantly felt Rusty's reaction. She stiffened, and I knew it.

I knew me being me at this level, making this kind of money, dealing with the deal-making men from the biggest deal-making companies, me being me was now just a bit too much.

A bit too much ...

Rusty's massive house and her new office on Sunset Boulevard, quite the addresses both of them, things were changing, it was the beginning of the end.

I moved again, from Bel Air to an apartment just off Wilshire Boulevard, and we got another huge deal — a national radio show.

Rusty and I were living in very different worlds, and that radio show was the last thing we did together.

I was breastfeeding my newborn baby. My third and last child. At 40 years old, I adopted my son, because I wanted to have another baby, I wanted to help young women, the birth mothers of the world, and I wanted his teen brothers to know what it is to have a newborn baby and what it takes all the years that follow.

His adoption story is a book within a book, but I must acknowledge here because it's oh, so obvious: breastfeeding an adopted baby? Yes.

One of the last things we did during whatever radio promo trip we were on, was to meet with a group of breastfeeding mothers whom I paid to donate breast milk for my son.

I paid $5,000 a month for breast milk he desperately needed, worth every cent, and I only could because I had the money and the notoriety to. I was only just beginning to live a totally different life.

Every day it was me, with my newborn baby in the studio doing a live radio show and Rusty on the other side of the glass with the men in suits. With them, not me, never happened before.

Months into doing the "Susan Powter Radio Show," I was asked to do a meeting with a potential huge sponsor to sell them on the show.

I remember walking up those massive stairs towards his office knowing I couldn't tell him it was a great show, and he should invest in it, because it wasn't.

The End of Rusty and Me...

We were at another big meeting in one of those massive glass buildings on Avenue of the Stars, and in the middle of the meeting, during a discussion about some production issue, one of the men leaned forward and said, "Hey, Rusty, I think a couple of your other clients can help us with this ..."

Other clients? She knew in that instant that I knew. We finished the meeting and before we even got to the car, outside in the courtyard I asked her directly, "Do you have other clients you've been working with without telling me?" Before she answered I knew, and I walked away and didn't speak her name for years.

I went home and immediately sent an email that read: "RPR and Associates and/or Rusty Robertson no longer represent Susan Powter or Stop The Insanity!"

I sent it to all of them, the CEOs, the heads of Simon and Schuster, Time Warner, Nexstar. One email, and I was done. One paragraph, and I severed it. I knew what a shock it would be when I sent it because of who I'd sent it to: everyone.

She called right after screaming at me, "How dare you, I made you, you would never have been anything without me," and I hung up on her and didn't speak her name again. Then I moved to Seattle.

Seattle...

Years before on a business trip in a limo on the way to the health food store to get the food I always got when we were traveling, I saw people jogging around a lake in Seattle, and I thought I could live here.

I rented a houseboat in Seattle to look around the city and find a house to rent, and I found one, the Wallingford House.

I think the rent was $5,000 a month, I couldn't tell you exactly, but I loved it. It was an old Seattle home in a lovely neighborhood years before any and all of the massive tech that is Seattle today moved in. The Seattle before-anyone-cared-Seattle.

It was just down the street from one of the best local bakeries in town and a few miles from the lake I had seen people jogging around years before.

I was raising my last child, photographing home births, and only just thinking about writing another book. I'd left L.A., left Rusty, left Stop the Insanity! and I never looked back.

I never thought about any of it again for years, until the writing of this book, actually.

From my attic office in that old house, I ended what had been 17 years of pretending to be co-parenting, which was actually me financially supporting their father to be a father.

From the landline (I need to explain in this day and age, not so long ago) speakerphone with the boys listening, I told him I was done. The boys were old enough to choose the relationship they would have with him, and I never spoke to him again.

Leaving L.A. was the beginning of me working grassroots, getting back to how it all started: teaching an exercise class in an old elementary school basement three times a week that I drove to in my VW Bug.

Way back at the beginning of it all at the second studio, as the deals were coming in, the corporation (otherwise known as Jerry) bought me a Lexus.

Not a car I asked for, needed, or would ever buy for myself, and when I was presented with it in the parking lot one day, maybe after the first few "Home Show" segments, and I when didn't gush with gratitude, Jerry was offended. I didn't "appreciate" his gift enough.

All I wanted and was going to buy for myself was a renovated VW bug, and guess what car I bought years later the minute I moved to Seattle?

Three times a week I'd drive (and I drove that thing into the ground) my VW

Bug, with my baby in his car seat and my aerobic sound system set up so I had the best music, and I did. It was quite a setup then, not so long ago, no internet need I say again …

I was making a living teaching exercise classes and I also taught private cooking classes from my kitchen. That's where I met Maryann, my dear friend 30 years later (whose name I still spell incorrectly — an inside joke) my friend who reminded me recently about our first cooking class, our introduction.

I was very much still Susan Powter then, as obvious as daylight, I'd only just walked away from Stop the Insanity! I was teaching and writing my next book, but I wasn't in the media or on TV. I changed the spotlight of my life to me, my kids, my work, my passions, which meant I disappeared. And I did.

One day Carolyn Reidy, CEO of Simon and Schuster, called to tell me they could not publish my next book because my ex-husband had threatened to sue, including it in his alimony lawsuit, and then she said, separate from that slight annoyance:

"Susan, do you know the last check we sent was for one million dollars, and do you know who we sent it to?"

"I did not," I answered.

"I assumed so" was her response ...

From there the financial shock waves kept coming, once I realized how much control I had given up of every contract, residual, whether I ever got a penny from any or all of my work. I had allowed someone to control it all, and not because I'm stupid, I'm not. Because I totally trusted, and I shouldn't have.

It's hard to describe the feeling of having just left everything as massive as Stop the Insanity! was and moving to Seattle with my family, but I'm writing a book now so, I suppose I should try.

Within a very short time after that email I sent, I never thought about it again. Never. I never thought about Rusty or the business again. Some, most, would call it emotional compart-mentalizing, but I can tell you that's not what it is. It's me.

It's me. When I know I know, and there's nothing more I need to know once I do. Whether it's Christmas or Rusty, when I know the truth I'm done, and I never look back.

There was still some money trickling in. I have no idea how much or from where. I still had one lawyer (out of more than I can count) left and a financial person handling basic bills, so whatever my monthly expenses were at the time, I know it was thousands, many thousands, less every month than a few months before.

It was after moving to Seattle, beginning to live my grassroots life, that I also found out the way the business had been being run, managed, handled for years.

Every check that came in was split 50/50. No contract, no questions asked (unfortunately) by me, ever. Ten percent is what managers get, but here's the kicker, at the very least to my heart.

It turns out the bills were being paid out of, being managed from, my 25 percent. And when you're

— meeting and meeting

— flying

— hoteling

— lunching

— deal-making

— office-spacing

— TV-showing, it's a lot ...

When millions of dollars are coming in, and that becomes more important to the person running it all than the organic, most-fun-we'd-ever-had-in-our-lives, when two women making it — what was always the most important thing to me — no longer mattered, it started to die.

My money was being hemorrhaged, and no, I didn't ask. I never asked to look at the bank balances, never asked to see what was going where.

I totally trusted my manager and all the lawyers, accountants and financial people I was paying to do what they were being paid to do. I was working around the clock.

My mistake, I not only take full responsibility for it, I've paid the highest price for the last 25 years because of it, because I did not check them all.

I was in no way living extravagantly in Seattle. I was teaching, making a few thousand a month and raising my baby. I was working and letting the dust fall where it may because I knew I'd never stop working. I knew I had plenty left in me and I was thrilled by what was, only just, happening with the internet.

I wanted to be interactive. Direct from me to you. Downloadable, i-Podable. I wanted it to be real. I wanted less produced, more me.

The fallout from me leaving was big and long, nobody could believe it, and everyone wanted to know what in God's name had happened.

I never spoke about it and was very happy out of L.A., taking early morning walks with my baby to the top of the hill to the coffee shop, strolling back and working on what I wanted to do.

I had written the books, done the speeches all over the world, made the appearances, shot the videos, held up, entertained, and pitched 80 thousand meetings. It wasn't that I was tired from the work, not at all. I was horrified at being lied to and at having my money stolen.

I knew my message, my brand had to grow, there was so much more I had to say. The last few years before I left, every project connected to me, every huge corporation making millions of dollars off of me, bit by bit they censored everything I did.

They produced me out of me.

Just look at the clothes I wore on that TV show — leisure suits and pearls? I've never put a pair of pearls on in my life, not to mention a leisure suit.

And my exercise videos, ask any of the thousands of women who've taken a class from me if I've ever worn a leotard to teach or sneakers.

I've never put a pair of sneakers on in my life but, you can't do that Time Warner said, you have to wear sneakers to teach aerobics, or they'll sue us.

"Oxygen, the only thing you can't live without for more than five minutes. Hold your breath and see what happens," I said, and "Oh no, no; you can't say that someone will do it and die, and we will get sued." "Anyone that stupid needs to hold their breath for five minutes," was my response.

It was a different time. A few corporations controlled the world. Three networks owned it all, and cable was just a nutty idea.

"Nobody's going to watch a channel that broadcasts news 24 hours a day," that's what they said about CNN. What was not that long ago is a lifetime ago.

It's a completely different world, everything, every industry has changed at the speed of light, it's called the internet.

I was in meetings at the height of Stop The Insanity! talking about producing my own products and selling them directly to my customer — the way everyone shops now — and I was told "People will never use their credit cards to buy anything on the internet, ever."

Just a taste of what I left behind when I left Rusty, L.A., and Stop The Insanity!

From that house in Seattle there was a love affair. A love affair with a journalist I met at a coffee shop who asked for an interview. A passionate love affair, never sexual, the best kind: a love affair of the mind, of books.

Reading them out loud for hours some days. Highlighting, dog-earring, life-changing from them, the women, we read all of them.

We did the interview, exchanged emails, and since she was an editor and I was thinking about writing a book, of course she moved down the street from me, and for a few beautiful years we worked together.

From there, a move to a cabin in the woods on an island off Seattle, and my life changed. I was getting closer to the way I've always wanted (still do) to live.

I was raising my last child exactly the way I wanted to raise him, and women. I was living around them, loving them, still paying any woman who could do a job I needed done, women.

That's how I went from Stop The Insanity! million-dollar deals and L.A., to a totally different life. And yes, I disappeared.

I disappeared according to a whole lot of people who'd bought my books, my videos, the amazing women who showed up, in force, to every live event, according to them I fell off the face of the earth.

It's been years since the millions were rolling in, even if only a very small percentage got to me. That's the story of that, but there's another story.

Uber Eats...

Yes, I'm writing a memoir, Em, from a kitchen counter in Las Vegas so many years later.

I'm still delivering after nine years.

Getting congratulatory confetti bursting texts from Uber Eats for my 4,000th delivery. I only recently (a year maybe?) started Uber Eats full-time because I got fired from Grubhub last year, which shook me badly.

I worked full-time with Grubhub since they started in Vegas when they had an office on Dean Martin Boulevard. When there were human beings you could talk to, way back in that day.

Delivering 8-10 hours a day has begun to really affect me this past year. Physically my shoulder, my foot, my knee, all on the right side of my body, they hurt.

My foot from being frozen on the accelerator and brake for hours a day for years, my knee from walking up and down thousands of apartment steps, and my shoulder from pulling the steering wheel for years.

Work-related injuries like a trucker or what went through my mind; like tennis elbow on a professional tennis player, obviously two worlds colliding.

It exhausts me, it defeats me now. The monotony, the waste of daily living that it is, that I know it is every minute of every day. Enough years have passed and not a thing has changed.

I feel it more now sitting in a parking lot waiting for the bell to ring for an order to come in when I need $80 for the day so badly for whatever bill is due. It's the math that never works, it can't.

— $80 a day.

— $20 for food: breakfast/lunch/dinner.

— $15 for gas for two shifts.

Which leaves $45 a day.

— $315 a week.

— $1260 a month, $1400 in a good month.

— Rent $800 when I first rented, up now to $980.

$980 a month rent which leaves next to nothing for everything else: phone, electric and on it goes.

There's never anything left, let alone if/when something happens — and it does. And what happens to me, to you, to everyone living this way when it does is indescribable.

It corrodes your being, it has mine. When I have to call my son for $20 to patch a tire, having lost the morning shift knowing I have to work until 7 p.m. to make up for it, it's crushing.

It is so far beyond just the dynamics of my family changing, it's what it's done to me, it's the physical reality of being a 60-plus-year-old woman delivering for Uber Eats.

I know I don't have all the time in the world left. Yes, I have more energy than anyone, I always have. It works wonders on huge platforms, with large crowds of people, but it turns inward when there's nowhere for my energy to go. My whole life this energy has been polarizing, just a bit too much.

I'm writing my story now simply because I can. I have a kitchen to come home to in a quiet, clean place. A counter to stand at, and as old as this computer is, I can use it and can, only recently, see the screen. That walk from the welfare office, not for nothing, for glasses to see.

I am very grateful to be anywhere other than Harbor Island, yes, but it's not the only thing I am. I am equally horrified, shocked, stunned and reminded every moment of the day how far away my life is from, not only what it was but from, the most basic everyday life I see people living all around me, and it has affected me. It crushes me, sometimes for days at a time.

I'm very grateful to be in a better place but shocked that I'm sleeping on a blanket on the living room floor with less than the average dorm room.

I'm so proud of this body of mine that gets up at 4:30 every morning to be in a parking lot, waiting for the bell to ring for an $8 order at 5 a.m. every day.

I'm very proud of how many years it's been that I've turned walking up and down stairs to drop off an order into gratitude for the movement and exercise.

I'm so grateful for this amazing body, proud and equally scared to death. It's frightening the waves of fear when I think of my reality; a woman in her 60s with nothing.

In the last 10 years I've worked every job you could imagine. I cleaned houses when the cleaning apps just started. I've been a prep cook in too many restaurants to count.

I was fired from a counter job in a small restaurant, a job I drove miles to and really needed, when the owner Googled me and found out who I was. I've worked seasonal work in the kitchen at a marina living in employee housing.

I've worked every job imaginable and a few impossible to imagine; months on the road working every state fair in the country as the head fryer in the fried lasagna tent. Don't ever tell me I didn't join the carnival, because I did.

I was thrilled to be able to deliver because it offered me the privacy to do everything I've done behind this wheel for years.

Died over and over again.

Resurrected over and over again.

Picking myself up by my bootstraps every time the waves of shock, fear, and knowing there's no way out of this. What will I do when the car breaks down again? What if I get sick? What if I get hit by one of these idiots on the road and end up ...

I work every day. My schedule has stayed the same for years. I'm up and out by 5 a.m. to get breakfast orders, mostly Starbucks and McDonalds.

I work very early mornings because the roads are different, it's all just beginning and it's not as jolting. I see all the early Vegas morning things, people, living.

I know what corners they live on, the convenience store parking lots they're organizing their shopping carts in. I see the world go from dark to light and watch everyone with normal lives wake up and start their days while I sit in parking lots waiting for a bell to ring.

Years of knowing the routes, restaurants, the staff; every holiday, every day. I am grateful, yes, but ...

It sucks the life out of me. It erodes, it's destroying me, no matter how hard I work. My biggest fear, of course, is not being able to deliver, to make day pay, to be able to sustain even this.

Getting sick. Never being able to get out of it at 65 is real, and living like this for years is what had me pulling into an urgent care parking lot and sitting for two hours in case I needed to get to a doctor fast, something was wrong and I was scared.

It was my heart. Never in my life have I felt my heart thumping through my chest the way I felt it that day. I don't have panic or anxiety anything, and if stress could kill me it would have years before this.

I went home that afternoon and lay down flat on my back, I couldn't turn onto my right or left side because my heart was pounding. I honestly thought before I went to bed, I might not wake up tomorrow. I wondered how long it would take for anyone to figure out I was dead.

It would be days before anyone came to check. I wished Em were still here because if I died, I knew she wouldn't leave my side, she'd sit with me until they found me.

The next morning, I woke up glad to have, same time, same schedule, 5 a.m. for the breakfast shift, but by 10 a.m. I had pulled into the hospital emergency room parking lot. I called my friend in tears, and said, "It's my heart, something's wrong with my heart."

The urgency in her voice was clear, she prompted me to walk into the emergency room immediately and I did. She told me a few weeks later that her first thought was, "Shit if something's wrong with her heart, we're all screwed."

I was hesitant to walk in, not for the "women put everything but themselves first" reason, no. I was hesitant to walk in because I had no money to pay for what I know are medical bills that ruin people's lives. And what was I going to say, my heart is pounding out of my chest?

I was hesitant to walk in because the medical system is the last maze I ever want to get tangled in, but what if I was having a heart attack? A 65-year-old woman under monstrous amounts of stress, isolation, sadness, and shock, it was perfectly possible.

They were terrific. It was a new hospital, nobody was in the waiting room and as soon as I told the front desk woman what was happening, three doctors ushered me into an examination room and started taking blood and hooking me up to monitors to see what was going on.

I was so grateful to be there knowing that if something happened, I wouldn't be alone and rotting for days.

I looked up at one of the doctors and said, "If something happens to me, please don't let them take me." "Who are they?" the doctor asked. "The morgue people. Don't let them or the funeral industry get their hands on my body, it's the final patriarchal earthly profitable abuse and I don't want to be their victim. I want to be composted."

He actually seemed to understand what I was saying, and then I just relaxed and let the doctors do their doctoring.

Turns out my blood pressure had spiked through the roof, never, ever happened before. They drew more blood, hooked me up to an EKG, gave me IV meds to see if my numbers changed enough to release me and told me they wanted to hold me there for a few more hours to decide if I needed to be admitted.

I left with prescriptions for one month, of more pills than I have ever in my life, and with a very clear message, "You need to see a cardiologist immediately," and I went home.

I needed a cardiologist,
and I had no insurance.

I haven't been to any doctor in well over 20 years. The last doctor's appointment I remember, I can't. I'm not a pill taker, not at all. I had to write down every pill I took every time I took one because ODing on blood pressure meds was not something I needed to add to this mess.

Immediately I started calling doctor's offices between deliveries and I was horrified. It was the first time in my life that I needed a doctor (other than a dentist, a whole other story) and couldn't get one when I needed it most.

There's not much more important to your health than your heart, and without the privilege of enough money to pay for medical care, without a private doctor, without what the majority of people live without every day, I couldn't get a cardiologist. It was also my first time being a 65-year-old woman calling doctor's offices.

Women and the AMA...

I can get you all the stats, I've read the books for years, but I don't need to. Because, if you are a woman and have ever had any interaction with a doctor of any kind for any reason, you already know.

Without knowing one statistic you've been treated like an idiot. You've been ignored. You've been disrespected. You've been, fill in your own blank, because you have been.

What was happening to me sitting in those parking lots between deliveries, trying to get a doctor's appointment was nothing I didn't know is real. What was shockingly real was that it was happening to me.

I was already caught in every financial trap possible and unimaginable — no credit, no savings, no way to make more than $15 an hour — and now, I was getting sick?

Something was wrong, and I couldn't get medical care. Impossible to believe. Is it harder to be caught when you know what you're caught in? Yes, it is.

Sitting between deliveries calling those massive corporate medical monstrosities, what health care is in this country, infuriated me. The minute they hear no insurance there's no chance of getting an appointment.

The only corporate conglomerate doctor's offices that I could get an appointment with was five to six months away. One woman asked me three times how to spell Susan.

Their system of having to have a primary-care physician to even make an appointment of any kind made it more difficult for two reasons: first, the drastic shortage of primary-care physicians in America and second, I didn't have one because I'm healthy.

What should be rewarded, should be the norm, which should be exactly what you want to hear if health has anything to do with what they're talking about, but it isn't, and I knew it.

I needed insurance.

Social Security...

My friend asked if I had applied for Social Security, I'd just turned 65. Not something I'd ever thought about (not turning 65, Social Security) but I was totally focused on getting insurance and that was the way to get it.

I can't fill out a form, literally. I can do a lot of things, but when it comes to forms, tests, required bureaucracy paperwork of any kind, I put the pencil down and sit there.

Just like I did from sixth grade on, literally. I put the pencil down and sat there and failed the tests.

I could never understand what they were asking, and I thought it was ridiculous. I always did, I always will.

I failed my driver's license written test over and over again. Only one of the reasons I'll never let my license expire — I won't be able to pass the test.

I have a visceral response to anything bureaucratically required, it's a very real energy thing, and it's always a disaster unless someone does it for me or with me.

I would not have Medicare today if Maryann hadn't spent two days on the phone with me walking through every step of what is one of the worst bureaucratic messes: Social Security.

We spent two days online filling out forms answering questions I had no idea the answers to.

What city my father was born in? Australia 80 years ago, how in God's name would I know that? Parents' birthdates?

No idea. What year? No idea. Name of, date of, address of? No idea.

Never having changed my last name for two marriages saved me. Who keeps their divorce papers 30 years later and why? Date of divorce? How and why would I know that? Lawyers handled it both times. I never saw a sheet of paper.

"Do you know your mother's birthday?" I asked my friend, as if it were perfectly normal to have no memory, at all, of even one birthday celebration. "Yes, Susan," she said gently, "most people do."

Obstacle after obstacle, back to the beginning of filling everything out again and again. Scanning my Social Security card (it was beyond a miracle I had it), proof of address, scanning my face, time after time, having no idea what the glitch was. Starting from the beginning again and again.

Two days later they still couldn't verify me as me, even though they had every piece of information about my life after I had scanned and submitted every detail. Without explanation, "We cannot verify you as you."

I am computer literate, and I had a very computer literate, as in 35-years-in-the-legal-world — friend doing it with me and still it was utterly ridiculous.

I don't have to write another word about the bureaucratic maze that any and all government everything is, everyone knows it is. It's horrible and made even worse when you need medical care, it's disgusting.

"Thank God you were famous," my friend said to me many times over the course of two days as she Googled me to get the most basic answers to questions about my life.

Two days on the phone and online. My very first Zoom call ever was to Social

Security to verify me as me. The first woman, who so obviously hated her job (could you blame her) hung up on me three times as if it were an accident.

Then a call with a young man who within seconds verified me as me and told me I would be getting a notice in the mail about getting my Medicare and Social Security check. I have no idea what it was that finally verified me as me, but it did and I am, and I got it.

Insurance was all I was thinking about at the time, hardly believing I would be getting a check every month. I had insurance, and I immediately made an appointment with a cardiologist, which I got for a few days away as opposed to six months.

Insurance...

Me going to a doctor is like me landing on Mars. Everything about it from the parking lot, I was stunned at how packed it was, to the waiting room, to being in a room with a doctor.

I was so uncomfortable in that waiting room. The filling in of forms, again, not my thing. It was packed with very sick, younger than me, seniors. I didn't belong there, I couldn't believe I was sitting there, but I had insurance!

I was still worried about the amount of the co-pay as I walked up to the window with my forms filled out. It was $35 and I had $50 in my account from deliveries the day before, which left $15 for food and gas for the day to get back to delivering right after to make up for the morning shift I'd lost. But I had insurance!

I just wanted to see what my numbers were and find out if anything was wrong with my heart. So much has changed in the last 20 plus years when it comes to a doctor's visit and certainly when you go from private doctors (all my life) to mass doctoring.

My first appointment was to get my blood pressure taken and chat with the doctor who the minute he walked in I could feel he had walked in and out of every room up and down that hallway for years. Same old, literally, same old.

He gave me more pills to hold me over until the next appointment to get an echocardiogram, which was the only reason I came to see a cardiologist, to get the next level of the EKG they'd done in the emergency room, scheduled for a week from then.

My second appointment was for a 45-minute scan of my heart in a room with a female tech about 50-something years old. Forty-five minutes lying in the dark hooked up to sensors as she scanned my heart, and we started talking.

You sound like ...

Stop The Insanity!, she remembered and she was lovely. We spent the hour with me talking nonstop about what she should do with her expertise, her many years of heart monitoring, patient support, watching what happens because of the all-American lifestyle. I literally laid out her new online career and she was all about it, thrilled.

I told her do a blog. As a mother. As the expert you are. Talk to women about what you've seen, what you know, what they can really do to prevent living with the horrible consequences filling your office waiting room, parking lot, and adjacent hospital.

Show them how they can make real changes in their daily lives while they are raising children, working overtime, doing it all; how they cannot end up in these offices. It was a fabulous echocardiogram. Nothing at all wrong with my heart.

The next, and last, appointment I went to a few weeks later, I asked where she was and they said she had quit, swear. Working her blog, I'm sure.

I went to a total of three appointments. My blood pressure went back to well below anything the AMA calls normal. I took two months of blood pressure meds and no more, no need. Apparently, a mountain of shock, fear, and sadness can affect your heart, because it did.

And then, I got a check ...

I got a check at the end of April, two months after I'd been in the emergency room. A check that shocked the hell out of me when I looked at my balance at 5 a.m. the next morning, like I did every morning for years for the $80 I needed to pay whatever bill it was that day.

I checked my balance that morning and time froze. It shocked me. I could not believe what I was seeing. I knew it was coming. I was told it would be, but when it did, when I actually saw that money in my account, I could not believe it. It was, and is still as I'm writing this, life-changing.

I could not believe the balance I was seeing; $1,523 overnight, more money than I had seen in years, much more than the amounts I had said over and over again: "If only I had $200, $50, an extra $100 right now. If only I didn't have to make the phone call to ask for money from my sons for ..."

If only I had,
and I had $1,523.

It was a shock wave, a tsunami of instant relief, and just in case it was a mistake and there was never going to be $1,523 a month coming ever again, from that parking lot at 5 a.m. I immediately paid ...

— $80 phone, can't deliver without it.

— $200 car insurance, again, can't work without it.

— $980 rent, third on the list of what has to happen every month.

— $60 for storage, for the last five years — a whole other story of being desperately afraid of not being able to pay it every month.

— $60 electric, and I had over $100 left?

I couldn't believe it. I'm not sure whoever said money can't buy happiness, but they were wrong. That money, that moment, bought me much, much more than happiness.

It restored long-dead hope, energy, belief, and possibility. It has completely changed the daily drudgery, humiliation, and exhaustion of every delivery I've done since.

Simply knowing every order I delivered for the rest of the month wasn't just about catching up anymore, for a moment I was ahead for the first time in years.

For the first time I could save something, anything, and I did. I delivered like a fiend and stashed every penny away in an envelope in my closet.

— Deep breath

— Lifesaving

— A moment of relief

— I had a chance.

Social Security Check...

I get a Social Security check every month. I still live exactly the same $80-a-day living; nothing has changed except everything.

That $1,523 a month
has changed my life.

Every month as soon as that check comes in, I pay rent and put everything that's left into an envelope that I hide in my closet, taped and tucked into my old itchy, brown convent-school uniform sweater.

I have stashed every penny of the money left over from every check in a sweater I stole from the Dominican Catholic convent I was raised in, in Australia.

I stole it when I was on tour with Stop The Insanity!, at the height of Stop The Insanity!

The afternoon of my speech I took a limo to the convent I was raised in, and I walked the grounds. Everything was shut down, was it a weekend? I couldn't tell you, but I distinctly remember walking the grounds, going from building to building.

The music room, where the nuns taught me the love of piano by turning a ruler sideways and whacking me (every music student in an Australian convent knows) across the knuckles when I hit a wrong note.

The kindergarten room, where Sister Mary taught. A young, beautiful, guitar-playing nun, and the blind school where I stayed for two weeks while my parents were on vacation in Europe.

We were the family that had the nuns-over-for-dinner-once-a-week kind of convent connection. I walked all over those grounds and into as many buildings as I could, and I stole two things.

A rosary, one of those huge brown rosaries the Dominican nuns wear down the side of their whatever you call the very complicated rig they put on every day. I stole a rosary, and I stole a brown sweater. The same brown, itchy, mandatory uniform sweater that I wore.

I know I found the sweater hanging over a wooden porch railing as if dropped by a child and hung there by the nuns, but the rosary? I can't remember how or where I found the rosary.

Did I break into the nuns' quarters? It's quite possible. I can't tell you, but what I can tell you is that all these years later I still have a piece of that rosary, and my cash envelope is taped inside of that itchy brown uniform sweater that I stole.

That night when I walked on stage in front of thousands of women, one of the biggest audiences I've ever had, the first thing I said was, "Hey, guess what I did this afternoon? I stole a rosary and a uniform from the convent I went to school at," and they roared!

They stood, applauded, howled, and chanted; it was and is a moment I will always remember. We'd all been to the same Catholic schools; we all knew what we knew.

Every month when my check comes in, I stash the cash left over in my envelope taped to that sweater. If ever the word hoarder applies, I stash the cash, and bit by bit I'm saving everything I can just in case, and what's changed is everything. Everything ...

The "what do I do if" that everyone on the brink knows has changed to: I have a bit of money in the envelope when it does, which changes absolutely everything. I put that money away obsessively, just in case.

*In case I can begin
to dream again.*

Maryann recently said, "You manage hardly any money better than any of those financial experts who had their hands all over your money."

The envelope has changed everything without changing a day off or the same math that doesn't or never will work. It gives me the privilege of borrowing from myself when I need that extra $100 for whatever bill because it's been a slow week.

The envelope gives me the luxury of not having to go back out to work the dinner shift, exhausted and defeated when after six hours I've only made $50 of the $80 I have to make.

I can't tell you the most difficult or the hardest part, times, daily things because there are so many, so many months and years of them. But I can say without a doubt that after delivering from 5 a.m. to 1 p.m., having to go back out to deliver for the dinner shift every time is always one of the hardest, most defeating, almost impossible things.

Every time, whether it's at the height of a 114-degree summer afternoon or the middle of a dark winter afternoon/evening shift, I knew it was killing me.

That necessary third shift made me acutely aware that I was being beaten down, badly. I hate it. It makes me feel like I can't do this anymore, and that leaves me with the dreaded fear of, "If I can't do this, then what can I do?" which is the kick in the gut of, "I can't believe any of this is true."

It is hopelessness. It is real fear made worse with every birthday that passes. Now when I need the extra $40, I don't have to work the dinner shift. I take it from the envelope, make myself some lunch, ice my back, lie down, and I put the money back in the envelope within a few days of delivering.

The envelope money makes me proud of myself every time I count it. It makes 100-plus-degree, eight-hour days of walking up and down apartment stairs to deliver food less defeating.

I wouldn't say a spring in my step after all these years, my foot, knee and shoulder hurt a bit too much for a springy step right now, but it makes it less humiliating, demoralizing, and shocking because I have a bit of money, just in case.

I push on with one thought in mind, thinking about adding money next month to my envelope. I chant the amount in the envelope month to month.

$2,300, I chant it all day.

The daily fear is subsiding a bit. I know I could survive a week, or more, if day pay goes down, and it does. Day pay being my only option. I haven't been able to make it through to a weekly payout in years.

Day pay, no matter the fee they charge, is the only way I can live, which greatly decreases the, very short, list of work I can get. An impossible to believe truth, only one of thousands.

It'll take some time for the fear to be replaced with any assurance at all that everything could be okay, that there's a way out, that there may be a possibility it didn't destroy me.

Maybe I have survived the land mines of the last how long? More than 10 years of impossible to believe. It'll take a moment to believe that I may be able to, a very big blank to fill in ...

So there it is,
you know the story.

You know a few stories, all the way back to the story that still has a ring to it 30 years later: Stop The Insanity! Now you know what happened, how it happened and when it did but, apparently, that's not the whole story.

The "This"...

My editor asked me a question the other day, as I was finishing up my book. He asked, "How did this happen to you, Susan?" Not the circumstances, the obvious, bad management, the story told, the story you just read. He asked me how this happened to me.

How did this happen "inside your brain, in you, while you were, as it was happening — how did 'this' happen to you?" "This" is all I heard. The "how" you know, you just read it.

It's a very good question, fair enough from one of the best editors in the business, so yeah — but one question that would/could change everything I write (from now on, forever?) as I'm finishing up, filling in, working on the end of my book?

I couldn't have imagined the answer to one question would do what it's done. What is the "this" that happened to me? The "this" I haven't written, after having written everything — but apparently not the "this."

Instantly it made perfect sense. It's exactly why I started my book with a letter to Em, because from that place it got unimaginable — but what? My living conditions, no. You know it went from crazy to the carnival years before, so is that what happened to me? No, it's not.

It's not the money. I hadn't had money for well over 15 years. I've been working jobs beyond my wildest imagination for years. I haven't been that Susan Powter for years and years.

All that changed over the course of everything you've just read, and the million other stories I have. How "this" happened is obvious and may I say so myself and I may, well written.

The answer to "how" is bit by bit, over more years than I ever imagined possible, from one job to another, one more unimaginable than the other, less and less opportunity as the years pass.

A 55-year-old woman looking for work is one thing, a 65-year-old woman quite another. Health, as good as mine is; teeth, bones, everything gets worn out, tired, and it's scary as hell when it all starts to.

Beaten down again and again absolutely. But, I never stopped working, believing with everything left in me, every time I had the most remote possibility of making just enough money to, I worked hard, every day.

All of it frightening, all discouraging, every bit of it embarrassing, exhausting and shocking. All of it chipping away at me over the years certainly, but it didn't kill me.

That's not what happened to me. That's not what made me truly believe there was no way out. That's not what shamed and embarrassed me. From Hollywood to Harbor Island isn't what happened to me. The "this" that happened to me was the "this" that almost killed me.

Broke is one thing,
broken is quite another.

The money changed from millions to $8-$15 dollars an hour over the course of years and has been (I've been delivering for the last nine of them) $8 to $15 an hour on a good day, as of yesterday. So, what's the "this" if it's not the money, the daily living, the shocking changes?

The "this" that started to change me, my family, my whole world started with hiding. I started hiding. I stopped everything. I stopped everything because ...

— I couldn't afford anything.

— It was too painful to see everyone else doing everything, all the things everyone does.

— I couldn't contribute to anything or anyone in my family and every time I couldn't it was crushing.

— I started losing me, the Being, the woman, the mother, me.

That's the "this."

That's the "this" that happened to me. It took year after year, loss after loss, less and less hope or belief that it could ever change.

I still had/have more energy than most ever will — no matter what. I began to feel it turning inward, my energy with nowhere to go is deadly. I started to feel disease setting in, which made me acutely aware that even my energy, belief, and hard work couldn't beat this, it frightened me.

The hiding changed from working on the Strip to fit-in-hiding, sticking out like a sore thumb not the goal there, to laying-low-living in KOA hiding, Susan Powter living in a crazy camper with her dog, to delivering-food-hiding.

I hid for days after Louis Anderson recognized me, delivering his food. It was obvious he knew it was me, and he was so gracious in the way he acknowledged it without acknowledging it.

Hiding anytime someone recognized my voice — "Hey, you sound like that crazy woman on TV in the '80s" — it was the '90s people!

To hiding within my family.

I had been hiding for years through all the daily living, jobs, circumstances, but hiding within my family was a whole other level of disappearing, and it unmoored me.

As anchored as I have never been in my whole life, the only thing that rooted me was my family, me and the boys.

I started referring to myself in the past tense, which is where — the only time in the telling of this story — "ex-millionaire" comes in.

The fall, the failure, the shock is amplified when you "used to be," when you "used to have." It makes it harder, sadder, more shocking when I'm delivering and the engine light comes on with no chance of paying for whatever it is this time.

The "this" was shame.

It was embarrassment, feeling as if I didn't belong, and that started and ended with my children and me.

Of course I've been embarrassed many, many times, but I was never ashamed until as a mother I felt shame on a whole other galactic level.

As a mother, as the head of our family, as who I've been for more years than I've been anything else, and it meant the world to me.

Family Video...

I found a video the other day of my youngest son's 18th birthday. I had no idea I had it, and it's a miracle I do. The first few minutes of that video alone was a baseball bat to my heart, and it's the answer to the question, what is the "this"?

I was living in KOA, a trailer park. I cooked beautiful food. I had a torn-up floor and no running water much of the time, a public bathroom next door, and I was working on the Strip seven days a week trying to make more than $50 a day, but I wasn't ashamed then.

We had a great time, like the Kennedys playing football at Hyannis Port. We threw the ball on the tiny patch of grass behind the pod, we laughed, talked, and then we went for a music-blaring ride, and the boys dropped me off and went off together, a perfect day, a perfect family visit, my family — and it was the last one.

I still had my family. We were still us, even though I wasn't quite me. I felt very much held in the esteem my children have always held me in; our family, me and the boys. I felt respected, it didn't matter how many things had changed in my life, we were still us.

The baseball bat to my heart that I felt watching that video was the shame I didn't feel then, and the years of shame I have felt since.

After all the changes, losses, impossible to believe, it was me losing me, the Being, the woman, the mother:

— From fierce to embarrassed

— Strong to weak

— Grounded to unmoored

What we, my family and I had lost and were losing at the speed of light, every memory, every holiday, every important event, everything, shattered me. The space it created between us shocked me.

They stopped coming to me because there wasn't anything I could do. I went from the only head of my household always to having nothing to do with anything and having to ask for everything.

Not being a part of anything, huge things, major life events that will never be again, of course that was the "this" that I didn't think I could survive.

But I did survive it. I'm still surviving it, but it turns out the most important loss out of all the losses was and is me.

As I'm writing this, the money is the same, the slow healing has begun, and nothing has changed except me.

What's changed is everything, without anything having actually changed yet, or maybe ever. We'll see in the next six months when I launch my brand again because I'm about to and here's how.

You already know what my Social Security check means to me, what it's done for my daily living, my month-to-month, what the possibility of putting anything, everything away means to me.

That check, the breath it gives me every month, is the oxygen that has nothing to do with "the only thing you can't live without for more than five minutes." It's the oxygen available when the pressure is off, when there's a bit more space to take a breath. It's possibility and hope, and if you want to totally insult elephants, it's the elephant off the chest.

You know, I know you know, so yeah, it's connected to money. The difference $1,523 a month has made, the difference it would make for millions of people. But as of now my money hasn't changed, but everything in my life has.

Everything in my life has changed.

The way I look and feel has changed even though no clothes, no makeup, no anything has. I look and feel different. Getting up in the morning is totally different. Delivering in this sweltering heat, however many summers later, is different.

Every conversation I have with my children is different. There would be no better way to explain the seismic difference with my family, without a thing changing, better than to tell you the story of picking up a car a few weeks ago versus the last time I went to pick up a car.

Harbor Island, five years ago, five months waiting to work, the flight there, that visit, the drive back versus a few weeks ago, flying to pick up another car my son bought me five years later.

The flight up alone! Being picked up at the airport, the drive to my son's beautiful home, and what a welcome from my grandson and his mother.

A fabulous, jam-packed weekend trip. I couldn't have had a better, more healing for me, without a word being spoken, visit. I was me again, I had me to contribute. It's amazing what a bit of hope can do.

I was me again because of a few, out of nowhere, impossible (anything I'd certainly stopped thinking was possible years before) circumstances that happened in the last seven months, and the fact that the last 10 years didn't kill me, and they are not going to.

And Then, The Impossible...

So, from the hospital emergency room to getting insurance, and a Social

Security check, I started saving every cent. Did it put a spring in my step, absolutely!

And then, out of nowhere, I got an email, a request to do an interview. The first request for TV anything in years, and I immediately said no.

Absolutely not. No chance in hell, because there's no way I could.

How could I possibly do an interview? When? Just after my last Jack in the Box order? Nobody in their right mind would get in front of a television camera (at 65 years old) 30 years later with not-even-close to Botox anything.

No chance with only the last of my teeth left, do I need to add here, not even close to the fluorescent white all teeth are now, no.

No, with this hair that's been up in a bun for five years and is thinning, thinner than my as-thin-as-hair-could-be-always-was hair. It's the answer to the much-asked question, why I shaved my head back in the day.

I bleached and shaved my head every week for years, because the best my hair has ever looked, the only volume my hair has ever had, is when it's bleached/ dead.

I never for a second thought about doing the interview and, credit where credit is due, the lovely producer spent three months going back and forth and was willing to do whatever it took to make this interview happen, everything you could try this woman did, but no, no chance I was going to do it.

And then, I decided I would.

I asked the question WWJD? It's a question I ask often, what would Joan do? What would Joan Rivers do?

I met her at QVC years ago, me in the middle of a massive lawsuit with Jerry, fighting for my brand, my career, and

Joan beginning to rise again, and did she ever!

She told me about Sony and their lawsuits against her, she told me about losing everything in Hollywood. She told me about Edgar, she told me about her broken heart. She told me to hold on, fight like hell, and keep working. I loved her, I love her.

Years later I went to see Joan's documentary alone in a little theater on Wilshire Boulevard. I'll never forget the scene where she showed her blank calendar book.

"If my book ever looked like this, it would mean that nobody wants me, that everything I ever tried to do in life didn't work. Nobody cared. I've been totally forgotten." Joan Rivers

It struck me and stayed with me for years. I could never have imagined then and there that my life would be much more unimaginable than an empty calendar. I think of Joan all the time, I have since the day she died.

I decided to do the interview because I asked myself WWJD? And the answer was/is she would show up for work if work was offered, so I did.

I chose a date and told the producer I'd do it. I was so unsure that I could pull it off, I had no idea if I still had it in me.

I was so aware of my teeth that I lied to her about having to get dental work the week of the shoot so I could get them (and I did) to change their standard direct-to-camera-HD-in-your-face shot a bit further back, not right up in my face.

I told them I'd do the interview, and then, within days, the second out-of-nowhere impossibility happened. A few days before the interview, just after I'd dropped off a delivery, I got a text that read, "Susan Powter?"

The minute it came in, I called my friend to help me figure out who in God's name was texting me. When I saw it I had a visceral cold (bad acid trip) feeling that it was someone I'd just delivered to, who somehow, after years of delivering, had figured out it was me.

Why else would you say "Susan Powter?" As in the Susan Powter I used to be?

Who else would have my number but a customer I'd just delivered to, or the four other people who do? Nobody, and nobody who would simply text "Susan Powter?" It scared me.

I never for a second thought it could be a film producer interested in doing a documentary about me, but it was.

Maryann called him to see if he was a lunatic and then, don't ask me why because I have no idea what came over me, I told him I was doing an interview, the first since I didn't know how long, and if he'd like to meet, he could come and watch the interview, and we could have lunch after and talk.

My thinking was he'll see who I am, if I still am, for, what turned out to be a four-hour interview, and I'll know immediately if I'm going to tell him any or all of it. His immediate response was, "What time is your call time? I'll be there."

I left a few hours early on the morning of the interview. I left with a full head of foam, bright yellow curlers, not something I do.

A. Curl my hair, it's been up for years ...

B. Curl my hair ...

C. Have enough hair to curl ...

D. You get my point ...

I rolled my hair hours before my interview that morning, praying that when I took the curlers down (minutes before the cameras rolled) and hair sprayed the hell out it so that maybe I'd have a chance my hair would look okay, for just long enough to last the interview, and it did.

I wanted to drive by the Airbnb they'd rented to see what was happening; the film crew had arrived much earlier to set up. I wanted to drive by way before my call time, because ...

— I hadn't had a call time in years.

— Because I was scared that I was making the biggest mistake of my wasn't-trying-to-make-a-comeback-all-these-years-later life. Believe me when I tell you I wasn't for a second thinking of a "comeback" of any kind.

— Because I didn't know until the cameras rolled if I could do it, because, because, because, because ...

I had an hour and a half after I drove past, so I pulled into a parking lot a block away and I did something I'd never done. Certainly not 30 years later.

*I YouTubed my
first infomercial.*

Of course I'd seen it on TV in the middle of the night, years and years ago like millions did, but I had never, ever sat and watched it since, and certainly not 30 years (having forgotten long ago about it) later in a parking lot, on a cell phone, about to do my first interview in forever.

I almost didn't press play because I thought it would be embarrassing. I thought I would be ashamed of it, and more shame was not what I needed just before I walked into this interview.

I thought it would make the next few hours more impossible than they felt sitting in that parking lot. I sat in my car watching my infomercial, a lifetime away from everything that had been Stop The Insanity! — and, I loved it.

I was so proud of it.
It shocked me.

No, not proud of the hokey food set up behind me and the massive before and after blowups; no, all of that is schmaltzy, but I loved it. I couldn't believe what I had done on that stage so many years ago.

I loved the Bambi story, it's the truth; it's exactly what happened to me when I went to an aerobics class, in Texas, in the '80s, morbidly obese.

Sitting in that parking lot, I was so proud. Of course, it's so, so dated; my cut-off sweatshirt, those purple (never worn purple before that or since?) tights, I know.

But sitting in that parking lot just before my first interview in too many years to remember, I was so proud of it. It reminded me of a lot more than I expected it to remind me of.

It reminded me of me.

I was watching it just before my interview about the infomercial industry never for a second thinking it would remind me of me, but it did.

I didn't expect that, it shocked me and made me cry out of pride for that young woman so many years ago, watching it just before the interview, I remembered me.

After all of it — all the iterations of how and when I went from, to, how and when the money was gone, how and when it all happened — I knew sitting in that car there was an ounce of me left, and I could do the interview.

When I say what's changed is everything, I mean everything has changed because I have. I've changed because I know without a doubt now that the biggest loss, the only real loss in all of this, was and is me, and I haven't lost me.

I have changed because coming home after delivering and jotting down my story has turned into a book, my memoir, and I love it.

I have possibility for the first time in years. Purpose, plans, human interaction — all of it makes a huge difference and is much better to wake up to than nothing, year after year.

Yes, but nothing has changed as I'm finishing this book, the least of which is the simple plan I've been trying to get to for well over 20 years.

The simplicity that I had completely given up hope that I would even be able to get close to. I have no idea what's going to happen with the movie, I'm thrilled to be even typing the word movie, and filming it for the last seven months, working with the lovely young filmmaker, has breathed life into me.

The response I've heard from so many people who are excited about this story has given me hope that I can and will do my work again.

So, here's the plan ...

First and within the next few months, an RV. What do you think I'm putting the money in my envelope away for? An RV that I've desperately wanted for years. A home. Something I own.

I'm going to buy an RV with worse than bad credit and with as big a deposit as I can save by the end of this lease, fingers crossed. It will be my home, a place to be with no neighbors, no landlords, no living for nothing but rent as it goes up and up, no more.

I don't want a new RV or a big steel silver, brown, and grey recreational monstrosity, no. I want under 10 years old because I can't stay in RV parks if it isn't —

i.e., kicked out of KOA. I want no bigger than a 19-foot, one-person RV.

The first thing I'm going to do is paint the whole thing red inside and cover it in white X-mas lights and crystals, and then I'm going on tour.

I'm going on tour to
sell my book, this book.

It's not as if I haven't done book tours before, five or six of them. I've done book tours but never a book tour like this. I'm going on the road, in my RV/home atmospherically hooked up online. Morning, noon, and night internationally connected, my idea of heaven, and what I've been trying to do since as far back as everything you've just read.

A thousand years ago I said downloadable, iPodable, linkable, and now a few times a day, every day, I'll be ...

— Split-screenable

— Duetable

— Reelable

— Instagramable

— TikTokable

— Live, morning, noon, and nightable, it's my dream.

Direct from me to you is what I said when I was trying to explain to the ecommerce-is-an-impossibility suits way back in the '90s.

And now, without having to explain it to anyone, I'm about to do it. We'll see how it works out, won't we, because I'm going on a book tour, kids!

I'll be on tour in the next few months with the book I am the most proud of. The book I own which represents the changing of the guards of all the corporate conglomerates I was up against in the '90s. I wrote this book like I've written all of them. But this time I own it, like I owned none of them.

I didn't have any control of what they ended up looking like, sounding like, being distributed and marketed as, not to mention the audios, videos, speaking tours, TV, radio, and on it went.

It's a whole new (internet) world now and I couldn't be more excited about it.

CHAPTER 2

I have a few more months left on this lease and then I'm going, so ...

I'll see you out there!

About the Author

Google me…

CONNECT WITH ME

https://www.instagram.com/susanpowter/

http://www.youtube.com/@stoptheinsanityoriginal

https://www.tiktok.com/@susanpowter

https://www.x.com/susanpowter

Made in the USA
Las Vegas, NV
22 March 2025

19948760R10105